THE SOUTH TODAY

The
South
Today

100 Years after Appomattox

Edited By WILLIE MORRIS

"The country that has a "history," dramatic, moving, tragic, has to live with it—with the problems it raised but did not solve, with the emotions that it leaves as a damaging legacy, with the defective vision that preoccupation with the heroic, with the disastrous, with the expensive past, fosters.
—D. W. Brogan

HARPER COLOPHON BOOKS
HARPER & ROW PUBLISHERS
NEW YORK

THE SOUTH TODAY. *Copyright © 1965 by Harper & Row, Publishers. Printed in the United States of America. All rights reserved. No part of this book may be reproduced in any form without permission in writing from the publisher, except by a reviewer who may quote brief passages in a review to be printed in a magazine or newspaper.*

FIRST EDITION.

First HARPER COLOPHON edition published 1966 by Harper & Row, Publishers, Incorporated, New York.

LIBRARY OF CONGRESS CATALOG CARD NUMBER: 65-21004

Contents

Foreword

In April of 1965, the 100th anniversary of Lee's surrender, *Harper's Magazine* published a supplement, *The South Today*, in which most of these essays, now revised and extended, were included. That issue provoked an unusually intense response from all sections of the country. One of the reasons, I think, lay in the dignity of the writing—its quality of controlled feeling, and the high degree of historical and literary introspection appropriate to the centennial of the ending of a war which still strikes deeply into our consciousness as Americans. The impact of that collection derived also from the closely connected events which brought the last days of the century since Appomattox to a close: the violence and bravery of Selma; President Johnson's moving appeal to Congress, with its momentous phrase—more determination, perhaps, than prophecy—"We Shall Overcome"; the march on Montgomery; and the swift introduction of the voting rights bill. A few weeks later Martin Luther King, the one leader since the 1950s among either race who has successfully galvanized national sentiment behind the Negro's grievances with tokenism and evasion, had moved his crusade from Selma, newest symbol of Southern recalcitrance, to Boston, seedbed of the old abolitionism.

To the rest of the country and to much of the outside world, the South today is more important and obsessive than it has been at any time in the last century. It is the most written about area of America, subject to the most apocalyptic interpretations; it is perpetually ending or coming into its own, with a character that oscillates from doom to mere eccentricity. In recent years its violent resistance to advances already established by the Constitution, statute or the Supreme Court has disguised the quickening pace of genuine social change. Television has made classic villains of its Connors, Clarks, and Raineys; their public brutalities have often resulted in further extensions of Negro rights. The events of Birmingham in 1963 focused on unequal treatment in public accommodations; some months later Congress enacted a civil rights law whose public accommodations section has now taken firm hold in most parts of the region. Selma in the spring of 1965 went further, dramatizing the inequities in the franchise, and mobilizing a Southern President and the Congress (including a number of Southerners) into enacting a sweeping voting law that would have been unthought of less than two years before.

At the same time, sensitive Americans all over the nation were becoming increasingly aware in these years of failings close to home, of social problems shaped by the Jim Crow tradition—*de facto* school segregation, riots, ghetto crime, urban poverty; these problems would not vanish with the complete destruction of Jim Crow throughout America, for they have been the result, as Bayard Rustin says, of "the total society's failure to meet not only the Negro's needs, but human needs generally." As Southern society in the last decade approached something of a national norm, the assignation of regional guilt and regional blame was becoming a more complex and subtle question than ever before. The South itself is less and less a monolith. Within the Old Confederacy there are mounting tensions and cleavages between the border states and the Deep South, and within the Deep South between city and countryside. My own background, for instance, embraces rural Mississippi and urban Texas, the two great extremities in the region, where the mode of life and the very consciousness of time itself are deeply in contrast; most of the contributors to this volume have directly experienced these disparities.

This collection of essays, while placing the last hundred years in their historical perspective, has as its main emphasis the South as it has become—the present relationship between South and North, between Southern white and Southern Negro, the moods and fears of the Southern people, the changing faces of the land and the cities. The contributors—writers, historians, journalists—were encouraged to draw upon their own experiences in describing the changes they have witnessed and the kind of future they foresee. With one exception, all the writers are native Southerners. Together, despite the inevitable contradictions, I think they have drawn a useful portrait of the present-day South.

One will find here a Southern white exile returning as a novelist to seek out the setting of an afternoon, years ago, of violent death; a historian showing how the North over the last century has helped buttress and condone segregation; a Southern conservative admitting that his fellow white "is just beginning to comprehend his own cruelties"; a Negro observing the changes among both races in his hometown; a student of W. J. Cash examining the pertinence after a quarter century of *The Mind of the South*; an editor arguing that Southern industrial growth, even with its advances, still makes victims of people. "The racial misery is within inches of driving us mad," William Styron writes; the Negro "may feel it is too late to be known, and that the desire to know him reeks of outrageous condescension, but to break down the old law, to come to *know* the Negro, has become the moral imperative of every white Southerner."

White Southerners and Negroes, it has been remarked by C. Vann Woodward, are the oldest, largest, and most incorrigible of the hyphenate American minorities. If there is a dominant human theme to this book, it lies in the personal, the institutional agonies, the subterfuges and cruelties which have in the past prevented or discouraged them from recognizing one another as fellow Southerners—as children and victims of a common past.

Willie Morris

New York City
May 1965

I

From the First Reconstruction to the Second

♦

by C. Vann Woodward

One difficulty in putting the century since Appomattox into satisfactory historical perspective is that it ended with a decade strongly reminiscent of the one with which it began. Events of the last decade have altered and are still changing our perspective on the rest of the century and much that went before. Looking back over the past hundred years and beyond, one will find no period of such concentrated change in the South since Captain John Smith disturbed the tranquillity of the aborigines at the dawn of the seventeenth century.

Admittedly that takes in a good deal of time and territory and depends much on what one means by change. It also provokes the skeptical challenge of how much change, in view of the South's determined resistance and fervent allegiance to the past, has really taken place. And to the historically minded the claim for the recent past as the high point of change immediately calls to mind other periods traditionally regarded as unrivaled peaks of revolutionary transformation. One of these is the period of Secession and Civil War, and another is its sequel, the period of Reconstruction.

Viewed realistically, however, both of those celebrated episodes may be described as revolutions that failed, elaborate plans for fundamental change that resulted only in temporary or superficial change. They were revolutions manqué. This is more obviously true of the South's hopes for Secession and Civil War than for the North's hopes for Reconstruction. No major collective effort in American history came such a cropper as the South's struggle to gain independence. As for Reconstruction, the argument is less self-evident. On the face of it the North had its way. The Rebel states were restored to the Union on the Union's own terms, the Rebels were penalized in various ways, the slaves were freed, the freedmen were made citizens, and the new citizens were granted the franchise and equal civil rights.

The catch was that these were changes in the law rather than in social realities. The sweeping new laws and Constitutional amendments were to some extent intended to result in social change, but in fact they rarely did. Other plans and purposes of Reconstruction, less firmly and formally expressed, included a redistribution of property and a reorganization of the South's economy to bring it into line with the needs and convenience of the North's economy. The Southern economy did lapse into a tributary and quasi-colonial relationship to the dominant region. But the Southern people of both races continued after Reconstruction to live much as they had before. If anything, old status lines were rigidified. Yet status change, we are told, is the essence of social change. The First Reconstruction, for all the political upheaval and the deep trauma it left on the mind of the South, was abortive and confined, a period of little basic change.

Alienated and Defiant

By comparison the Second Reconstruction is assuming the proportions of a galloping revolution. Like the First, the moral objectives of the Second are crosshatched with lines of economic disturbance that are only tangentially related. This time, however, the way people live, where they live, and how they make their living are changing massively and with unprecedented speed. In the single decade of the

1950s the South's urban population increased nearly as much as during the three preceding decades, and in the previous decade Southern metropolitan areas grew more than three times as fast as comparable areas in the rest of the country. The Negro exodus has lowered the black-white ratio to one in five and the South's share of Negro population to less than 50 per cent. In the meantime the percentage of the labor force employed in agriculture (more than 50 per cent in 1920) had dropped to 10 per cent by 1960, and employment in manufactures expanded faster in every Southern state but one than it did in the nation as a whole. Old cities took on new life, new ones sprouted magically, and the money rolled in. The old gap between Southern poverty and national wealth was not closed, but it was markedly narrowed. In these ways the South was shedding penalizing disparities and traditional distinctiveness, and becoming more and more indistinguishable from the rest of the country. By all the canons of economic determinism the South should at long last be swinging into the mainstream of national life, joyfully embracing the American Way.

Instead of this, the South since 1954 has been more deeply alienated and thoroughly defiant than it has at any time since 1877. In these respects the 1950s and 1960s were a historical flashback to the 1860s and 1870s. Once again the South was isolated, the last defender of a discredited and outlawed institution. It had lost its appeal to the conservative North, to the Constitution, to the President, and to Congress. Southerners automatically assumed hereditary roles and postures and repeated lines from the historic script that sprang to their lips from memory. Reconstruction legends, as Gunnar Myrdal remarked, are prime "symbols of regional allegiance." And recent events have evoked these legends as never before. The South has been reliving an old trauma.

An essential ingredient of resistance morale in the First Reconstruction was the legend of betrayal, a breach of faith. Having laid down their arms under honorable conditions of surrender, so goes the legend, the vanquished were then forced when helpless to submit to a dishonorable change of terms. The legend has its counterpart in modern charges of broken faith. It is not merely that the North has torn up the Compromise of 1877, but that it has compounded the betrayal by overturning successive reavowals in the *Civil Rights Cases* of 1883, in *Plessy v. Ferguson* of 1896, in a dozen party platforms of the Progressive Period, and in scores of time-honored accommodations, prerogatives, and rulings in Senate and House, in department and bureau, in Army and Navy, and in state and federal relations down through the second world war that had proclaimed and repeatedly acknowledged to the world that this country was dedicated to white supremacy and stood prepared to bring to bear federal authority to enforce it.

A graph of the South's rise from the misery of rejection in the seventy-odd years between the two eras of Reconstruction would start at the bottom in the 1870s. The line would describe a slow curve upward through the last quarter of the nineteenth century and level off at a relatively high plateau of acceptance through the first four decades of the twentieth. The long pull up from the depths of rejection anxiety left its mark on the Southern personality structure. The old image of the arrogant, mettlesome, overbearing Southerner was replaced by a genial, easygoing, deferential, and glad-handed Southerner noted for talents of compromise and accommodation. He was easier to accept and harder to resist.

The accommodations came in the form of concessions and retractions from above the Potomac, reconciliations between white men at the expense of black men. Once the admission was publicly made that all those fine-sounding, idealistic Civil War commitments to equality were impulsive, ill-advised, and not to be taken literally, the rest came without much difficulty. The sections had never been far apart on race policy, anyway, only on slavery. Once the country embarked on overseas imperialism and the rule of colored people beyond its borders at the end of the nineties in the Caribbean and the Pacific, little more was heard about the wickedness of Southern ways. The twentieth century dawned on a new era of harmony between the dominant whites of North and South, East and West. Civil rights beyond the color line became virtually a dead letter, Negro disfranchisement enjoyed federal approval, segregation was the law of the land, and progressivism was for whites only. The Southern Way had become the American Way.

And Then Truman

So it was that the South emerged from pariahdom and marched unchallenged into the progressive movement under the banner of white supremacy. It arrived with a sense of acceptance and oneness with the national temper such as it had not enjoyed since the Jacksonian period. The euphoria of approval and release from anxiety was enhanced by the Presidency of Woodrow Wilson, a Southerner even if he was of Northern residence. Relieved of the crippling obsession with race problems, now swept under the rug of national consensus, the old reform impulses that had been repressed in the Populist era burst out in the New Freedom to provide indispensable support for Wilson's domestic reforms. Identification with Wilsonian foreign policies came easy, and the South took the lead in supporting intervention, backing war measures, and sustaining the losing fight for the League of Nations. Regional identification with Franklin D. Roosevelt presented no insuperable problems, and for many Southerners he seemed another Wilson, the New Deal a replay of the New Freedom. And when Roosevelt turned from domestic reform to foreign crisis, as Wilson had done before him, the South was once more in the vanguard of interventionists and internationalists, rescuing the extension of the draft law, backing the war program with enthusiasm, and carrying through with the United Nations as if it were the final vindication of Wilson's League fight. "Internationalism" was thought to have found its home below the Potomac.

The South came through the second world war still wearing its feeling of acceptance and belonging, if anything more secure in its possession than before. This security was founded on nearly a half-century of experience in which the South had built up the expectation and assurance of continued national approval. Only with the expectations of that period in mind can one understand the outburst of rage, the hysterical shock of disappointment, and the cry of betrayal and bad faith that followed—the charge that the North had changed the rules.

There had been warning tremors, but the first real crack in the national consensus came when Harry Truman backed the recommendations of his Committee on Civil Rights at the Democratic

Convention of 1948. The implications were ominous and immediately apparent. This meant a return to principle, a shift from "uplift" to rights, from paternalism to equality, the breakup of compromises, accommodations, and concessions that dated back to 1877. The Solid South shuddered to its roots and split, and remains split to this day.

The radical phase of the Second Reconstruction really did not start until 1954, for until May 17 of that year segregation was still the law of the land. The *Brown v. Topeka* decision and its sequel in 1955 ended legal claim of white monopoly of schools and other civil institutions. Judicial reconstruction was supplemented by Congressional reconstruction with the Civil Rights Acts of 1957, 1960, and 1964, opening up one private door of exclusion and discrimination after another. And in 1962 *Baker v. Carr*, the decision on legislative redistricting, threatened the whole domain of rural white political privilege that sustained the white man's rule. In the meantime Southern whites witnessed what to their inflamed historical imagination was the flesh-and-blood materialization of ancestral nightmares that had troubled their sleep since childhood. Negroes at the ballot boxes, federal bayonets in the streets, a rebirth of scalawags, a new invasion of carpetbaggers, and battalions of abolitionists and Yankee schoolmarms in the form of Freedom Riders and sit-ins and CORE and SNCC and COFO.

The old regional syndrome of minority psychology and rejection anxiety had settled down on the minds of much of the South by 1954. In its grip debate and dissent were stifled. It is a mistake to dismiss the reaction as calculated or cynical, for it was often deeply felt and deadly serious. A besieged minority instinctively felt it could not afford the luxury of internal division. It was essential to close ranks, to set up an intellectual blockade. Looking out upon a world they felt to be critical or hostile, many Southerners yielded to impulses of withdrawal, to suspicion of all outsiders, and to fear of all outside ideas, movements, and opinions. In the extreme instance these paranoid impulses resulted in what Professor James W. Silver has described as "the closed society" of Mississippi.

In the modern revival of the Reconstruction melodrama, Southern voluntary defense associations outnumbered those of the original. The modern counterparts of the Knights of the White Camelia and the Ku Klux Klan included the White Citizens' Councils, White America, Inc., Grass Roots League, Inc., States Rights Council of Georgia, National Citizen's Protective Association, Individual Liberties, National States Rights Party, Society for the Preservation of State Government and Racial Integrity, not to mention the enfeebled revival of the Ku Klux Klan. With a license to lawlessness from responsible leaders who defied the law and denounced the courts, the hoodlum element and their allies in the constabulary laid about with club and gun and kerosene and dynamite sufficiently to lend realistic blood-and-thunder effects to the re-enactment of Reconstruction.

Southern politics of the last decade, fulfilling its role in the drama, became a game of historical charades, elaborate parodies of Confederate stratagems: nullification, interposition, massive resistance, Congressional manifestoes, filibusters, tickets of independent Presidential electors, calculated defiance of federal law, and north of the Potomac the mobilization of the concurrent majorities of the backlash, the new model Copperheads. Never did the South act more 'Southern," nor have more melodramatic actors for the standard roles—a Thurmond of South Carolina, a Faubus of Arkansas, a Barnett of Mississippi, a Wallace of Alabama. "I draw the line in the dust and toss the gauntlet before the feet of tyranny," declaimed Governor Wallace in his inaugural address. And the camera eye soon found him "standing in the schoolhouse door." Adolescent, to be sure. But millions thrilled to the sight, even in remote Wisconsin and Indiana and Maryland.

The search for a new compromise began early and with plausible expectations of success. Reformers have rarely been able to sustain the zeal of their followers much longer than a decade. Protracted enthusiasm is a terrible strain. Historically, all such sectional clashes had been resolved in the end by compromise. All save one. There was no compromise in 1861. But no one thought of resort to war in the 1960s, and few seriously contemplated military occupation as more than a temporary and rare expedient. The prospects for an accommodation were not discouraging. In far weaker circumstances, after a crushing defeat, years of military occupation, and extensive disfranchisement, the South had been able to negotiate on favorable terms a compromise that outlasted all the others, the Compromise of 1877. Why not another? Say, a Compromise of 1964? Governor Wallace was obviously thinking along these lines when he observed, "We used the electoral college in 1876 to get the federal troops off our backs. We can use it in 1964 to get the liberals off our backs."

This one might well become known informally and privately as the Compromise of Tokenism. It would assume, in the classical manner, nominal compliance without fundamental change. It might be thought of as a sort of Lincoln Plan for the Second Reconstruction. It was an old American tradition to appease reformers with impressive statutes and then neglect or forget about their implementation. After ten years of school desegregation at "deliberate speed" only 2 per cent of the Negro pupils in the old Confederate states were in schools with white children, and nearly half of those were in Texas. Yet all these states were now proudly marked on the newspaper maps as "desegregated." It was surprising how much approval and congratulation these minimal gestures won from outside. Perhaps token desegregation, Southern style, or perhaps de facto segregation, Northern style, would do. Or perhaps an ingenious blending of the two models.

Signals of reaction in North, East, and West were auspicious. The Supreme Court had fallen under severe attack for several reasons and in many quarters, including some highly respectable ones. The conservative press swelled the outcry. On the racial front Northern chickens began to come home to roost in disturbing fashion in the early sixties. For many years the Southern Negro exodus had been augmenting the big city slums until many of those cities had accumulated as large a percentage of Negro population as Southern cities—sometimes even larger. It now began to dawn upon those cities that this time Radical Reconstruction was going to apply to them as well as to the South, and they appeared no more eager to embrace it.

Trade unions set up an indignant outcry against Negro demand for admission. Employers bitterly complained against infraction of their freedom to hire and fire. Homeowners, organized for protection or aggression against unwanted neighbors, took ugly and violent forms of action. White parents demonstrated more numerously and noisily against integration than Negro parents did for desegregation. Militant defenders of "neighborhood schools" adopted extreme measures. Tensions over school integration began to run higher outside the South than inside. While legal segregation of schools was retreating more and more placidly by inches down South, *de facto* segregation and "resegregation" were gaining by leaps in some quarters up North.

The surge of national sympathy for the civil-rights movement (even when described as the "Negro Revolution") that sprang up in response to the demonstrations of 1963 and the savage reprisals against them in Birmingham and elsewhere began to recede rapidly. In the summer of 1964 mob violence raged in cities of the Northeast, most furiously in the black ghettos of New York, Jersey City, Rochester, Brooklyn, and Philadelphia. Looting, pillaging, and property destruction continued night after night beyond control in some cities. White reaction fed on these outbursts to whet the rising revolt of the Radical Right that was currently sweeping the country. "The Negroes have gone too far," was the cry. Here was the potential electorate of backlash Copperheadism that the Southern resistance had been looking for. Governor Wallace was scoring sensational successes among them. At the height of the reaction a determined minority succeeded in aligning the Republican party with the racist movement.

Had it been left up to the white man, North and South, the Second Reconstruction possibly would have already gone the way of the First—the way of compromise, conciliation, and appeasement into frustration and failure. It would have been the old story of white men resolving their differences at the expense of black men. The will was present on both sides, and incentives and opportunities abounded. But this time it was not left up to the white man. The Negro himself was a decisive participant, not an instrument of white purpose.

The Negro was not as fully enfranchised as he had been in the 1860s, but the voting power he did have was more strategically located. He was better led and better organized and, what was more important, the leaders and organizations this time were his own. And he was inspired by a new consciousness of power, supported more resolutely by his white allies, dedicated minorities in the North and smaller but important ones in the South itself, and he was conscious of an alert and involved world audience for his struggles instead of an indifferent one as before.

Johnson's Opportunity

It is too early to fix upon a decisive turning point in the fate of the Second Reconstruction, but it is not too much to say that its future was in considerably more doubt before the Presidential election of 1964 than after. The impact of the Negro vote in that election will long be remembered, and it may loom larger in long-term perspective. It was virtually unanimous in the South, unprecedentedly so, for General Grant scarcely polled the Negro vote so solidly as President Johnson. In the eleven Southern states, it clearly made the difference between victory and defeat in at least four states, Virginia, Tennessee, Florida, and Arkansas, and probably a fifth, North Carolina, as well. Texas was the only one of the eleven Southern states he carried with a clear white majority. The five Goldwater states of the lower South were those with the lowest Negro registration. And yet with solid Negro support Johnson won more than 51 per cent of the total vote in the old Confederacy.

Things could never be quite the same in the South again. The striking change is the sharp constriction of die-hard resistance to the lower South. The First Reconstruction had the effect of bringing the Border states into the South's orbit, making them more "Confederate" after the Civil War than before. The Second Reconstruction has had just the opposite effect. The Border states deserted early in the game and have drifted farther and farther away. Now the upper South along with Texas and Florida have defected as well. Ralph McGill has remarked that the "stark isolation" of the five Southern Goldwater states "may prove in the long run to be a necessary therapy," for they have now "so isolated themselves that they cannot fail to see how terribly and irrevocably alone they are."

Even so, the majority of states and the majority of voters in the old Confederate South are now on record in support of a President who has gone further ("nothing less than the full assimilation of more than twenty million Negroes into American life," he said) in public commitment to the protection and extension of Negro rights than any one of his thirty-four predecessors, including all those elected by what was once known as the party of emancipation and Negro rights. Moreover, he was one of their own, the first President of Southern birth and residence elected to the office in 116 years. That is a fact of profound if imponderable significance for the future of the Second Reconstruction. It was not of itself enough to win the votes of a majority of his fellow Southern whites. On the other hand, it was not enough to prevent the solid support of Southern Negroes.

The Negro vote is not tied to Lyndon Johnson, but it *is* tied to civil rights, and the only probable trend of Negro registration is up. All previous experiments of massive Negro participation in Southern politics—notably in Radical Reconstruction, in the independent party revolts of the 1880s, and the Populist revolt of the 1890s—have ended in polarizing politics along racial lines and isolating the minority race. Advocates of a new polarization of races have already appeared on Left and Right. Johnson has a greater opportunity than any native Southern leader since the Populists to forge a political union of the two races and prevent the racial polarization of Southern politics.

A testing time for Johnson's commitment to civil rights was not long in coming. Martin Luther King announced he would lead a march from Selma to Montgomery to dramatize the demand for voting rights on March 6, 1965. Disregarding Governor Wallace's order forbidding the march, some 650 people set forth and were brutally repulsed with clubs and tear gas. One Negro worker had already been killed and a white minister was beaten fatally in the streets. Thousands of sympathizers converged on Selma from all parts of the country. When Wallace refused to provide military protection after a federal court order assuring the right to march on Montgomery, the President promptly ordered out troops, marshalls, and the FBI in force. He then addressed Congress and the country in the most stirring speech of his career on Negro rights. Selma, he declared, was "a turning point in man's unending search for freedom." His words and tone left no doubt about the commitment of his administration to that search.

The President announced he would send to Congress a bill "designed to eliminate illegal barriers to the right to vote" and declared that "there must be no delay, or no hesitation, or no compromise with our purpose." It proved to be a tough bill, tougher in fact than any framed by the First Reconstruction to protect the Negro's right to vote. It banned the literacy test for registration where less than 50 per cent of the voting age population was registered and voted in the election of 1964 and authorized the use of federal registrars when necessary to enforce the Fifteenth Amendment. After some changes that tightened its provisions further, the bill was pushed through Congress in far shorter time than it had taken to adopt the three civil rights acts of recent years.

The Second Reconstruction has turned a corner. It is not yet out in the clear. It is likely to suffer setbacks and backlashes in the North and sure to meet new resistance in the South. But it would seem to be fairly out of the dark part of the woods in which the big sellouts of sectional compromise have traditionally been made. As halting as its progress has been, as cynical as tokenism can be, and as brutal as extremists still are, the Second Reconstruction has already scored up more achievements of durable promise than the First ever did. For all the fine idealism of the few and the impressive heritage of legislation, the accomplishments of the first round of Reconstruction were largely rhetorical. The freedmen continued throughout to knock at the back door for whatever opportunities were opened to them. And the whites, Northern as well as Southern, rarely unbent in their assumption of racial superiority.

This prognosis for the Second Reconstruction does not include the prospect of millennial fulfillment. It only suggests that the South is moving, painfully to be sure, toward an approximation of conditions in the rest of the country. It would be well to ponder those conditions soberly before leaping to naïve optimism about the South. The point at which token desegregation in the South merges indistinguishably with *de facto* segregation in the North falls somewhat short of utopian integration. But what of those "vast impersonal forces" such as industrialization and urbanization, referred to earlier, as working powerfully in the South? What of their "inevitable consequences"? There are indeed certain contradictions between smooth industrialization and racial reaction. Even an editor of Philadelphia, Mississippi, recently observed that "prospective industrialists will surely pass us by if we show signs that we won't obey the law. . . . They don't want trouble in their plants and among their employees." But racial felicity has not proved to be an inevitable consequence of the profit motive. There has been a good deal of urbanization and industrialization up North without impressive consequences of this character.

Even if the South moves more rapidly toward national standards, racial and industrial, it will still be destined to endure for a time the slings and arrows of rejection. It is back in the old limbo, nursing new bruises to pride and licking old wounds to self-esteem. The wounds are kept open by attacks that are just, as well as some that are less than that. The national press has license to use "redneck" and "cracker" in a way it is strictly and rightly restrained from using equivalent epithets for the other race. For the South is judged not by the gains that have been made in large areas of the region. Defiance makes the headlines, not compliance. The South is judged by what happens in Mississippi and Alabama. And what happens there surely provides enough odium for the whole region, perhaps for the whole country. There is, however, understandable complaint about how the burden of guilt is distributed.

Mutual Discovery

The South has lately had its "Epitaph" written and its "Mystique" debunked. The implication would seem to be that the South's disputed "distinctiveness" and Southern identity inhere essentially in retrograde racial policies and prejudices. With the gradual disappearance of these, Southerners are expected to lose their identity in a happily homogenized nation. Quite apart from the South's preferences, there are other reasons for skepticism in this matter. The South has long served the nation in ways still in great demand. It has been a moral lightning rod, a deflector of national guilt, a scapegoat for stricken conscience. It has served the country much as the Negro has served the white supremacist—as a floor under self-esteem. This historic role, if nothing else, would spare the region total homogenization, for the national demand for it is greater than ever.

Up to the time of the Second Reconstruction the Southerner who rejected racism looked mainly to the past to establish his regional identity. He looked to the collective experience of the Southern people with defeat and failure, frustration and poverty, guilt and tragedy that made his heritage unique in the nation. These dark, Faulknerian themes are not going to vanish in the light of the new day. They will continue to play a part in defining a Southerner. The Negro Southerner shared that heritage deeply without accepting it consciously, without even acknowledging fully that he was a Southerner. In the new era Southerners of both races are looking increasingly to the future instead of the past, to action instead of memory, to define who they are. In this new search for identity the Negro is fully engaged. In fact, he has taken the initiative and the white man reacts to him. Their discovery of each other will define a distinctively new period of Southern history and a new Southern identity.

II

This Quiet Dust

◆

by WILLIAM STYRON

> *You mought be rich as cream*
> *And drive you coach and four-horse team,*
> *But you can't keep de world from moverin' round*
> *Nor Nat Turner from gainin' ground.*
>
> *And your name it mought be Caesar sure*
> *And got you cannon can shoot a mile or more,*
> *But you can't keep de world from moverin' round*
> *Nor Nat Turner from gainin' ground.*
>
> —Old-time Negro Song

My native state of Virginia is, of course, more than ordinarily conscious of its past, even for the South. When I was learning my lessons in the mid-1930s at a grammar school on the banks of the James River, one of the required texts was a history of Virginia—a book I can recall far more vividly than any history of the United States or of Europe I studied at a later time. It was in this work that I first encountered the name Nat Turner. The reference to Nat was brief; as a matter of fact, I do not think it unlikely that it was the very brevity of the allusion—amounting almost to a quality of haste—which captured my attention and stung my curiosity. I can no longer quote the passage exactly, but I remember that it went something like this:

15

"In 1831, a fanatical Negro slave named Nat Turner led a terrible insurrection in Southampton County, murdering many white people. The insurrection was immediately put down, and for their cruel deeds Nat Turner and most of the other Negroes involved in the rebellion were hanged." Give or take a few harsh adjectives, this was all the information on Nat Turner supplied by that forgotten historian, who hustled on to matters of greater consequence.

I must have first read this passage when I was ten or eleven years old. At that time my home was not far from Southampton County, where the rebellion took place, in a section of the Virginia Tidewater which is generally considered part of the Black Belt because of the predominance of Negroes in the population. (When I speak of the South and Southerners here, I speak of *this* South, where Deep South attitudes prevail; it would include parts of Maryland and East Texas.) My boyhood experience was the typically ambivalent one of most native Southerners, for whom the Negro is simultaneously taken for granted and as an object of unending concern. On the one hand, Negroes are simply a part of the landscape, an unexceptional feature of the local scenery, yet as central to its character as the pinewoods and sawmills and mule teams and sleepy river estuaries that give such color and tone to the Southern geography. Unnoticed by white people, the Negroes blend with the land and somehow melt and fade into it, so that only when one reflects upon their possible absence, some magical disappearance, does one realize how unimaginable this absence would be: it would be easier to visualize a South without trees, without *any* people, without life at all. Thus at the same time, ignored by white people, Negroes impinge upon their collective subconscious to such a degree that it may be rightly said that they become the focus of an incessant preoccupation, somewhat like a monstrous, recurring dream populated by identical faces wearing expressions of inquietude and vague reproach. "Southern whites cannot walk, talk, sing, conceive of laws or justice, think of sex, love, the family, or freedom without responding to the presence of Negroes." The words are those of Ralph Ellison, and, of course, he is right.

Yet there are many Souths, and the experience of each Southerner is modified by the subtlest conditions of self and family and environment and God knows what else, and I have wondered if it has ever properly been taken into account how various this response to the presence of the Negroes can be. I cannot tell how typical my own awareness of Negroes was, for instance, as I grew up near my birthplace—a small seaside city about equally divided between black and white. My feelings seem to have been confused and blurred, tinged with sentimentality, colored by a great deal of folklore, and wobbling always between a patronizing affection, fostered by my elders, and downright hostility. Most importantly, my feelings were completely uninformed by that intimate knowledge of black people which Southerners claim as their special patent; indeed, they were based upon an almost total ignorance.

For one thing, from the standpoint of attitudes toward race, my upbringing was hardly unusual: it derived from the simple conviction that Negroes were in every respect inferior to white people and should be made to stay in their proper order in the scheme of things. At the same time, by certain Southern standards my family was enlightened: although my mother taught me firmly that the use of "lady" instead of "woman" in referring to a Negro female was quite improper, she writhed at the sight of the extremes of Negro poverty, and would certainly have thrashed me had she ever heard me use the word "nigger." Yet outside the confines of family, in the lower-middle-class school world I inhabited every day, this was a word I commonly used. School segregation, which was an ordinary fact of life for me, is devastatingly effective in accomplishing something that it was only peripherally designed to do: it prevents the awareness even of the existence of another race. Thus, whatever hostility I bore toward the Negroes was based almost entirely upon hearsay.

And so the word "nigger," which like all my schoolmates I uttered so freely and so often, had even then an idle and listless ring. How could that dull epithet carry meaning and conviction when it was applied to a people so diligently isolated from us that they barely existed except as shadows which came daily to labor in the kitchen, to haul away garbage, to rake up leaves? An unremarked paradox of Southern life is that its racial animosity is really grounded not upon friction and propinquity, but upon an almost complete lack of contact. Surrounded by a sea of Negroes, I cannot recall more than once—and then briefly, when I was five or six—ever having played with a Negro child, or ever having spoken to a Negro, except in trifling talk with the cook, or in some forlorn and crippled conversation with a dotty old grandfather angling for hardshell crabs on a lonesome Sunday afternoon many years ago. Nor was I by any means uniquely sheltered. Whatever knowledge I gained in my youth about Negroes, I gained from a distance, as if I had been watching actors in an all-black puppet show.

Such an experience has made me distrust any easy generalizations about the South, whether they are made by white sociologists or Negro playwrights, Southern politicians or Northern editors. I have come to understand at least as much about the Negro after having lived in the North. One of the most egregious of the Southern myths —one in this case propagated solely by Southerners—is that of the Southern white's boast that he "knows" the Negro. Certainly in many rural areas of the South the cultural climate has been such as to allow a mutual understanding, and even a kind of intimacy, to spring up between the races, at least in some individual instances. But my own boyhood surroundings, which were semi-urban (I suppose suburban is the best description, though the green little village on the city's outskirts where I grew up was a far cry from Levittown), and which have become the youthful environment for vast numbers of Southerners, tended almost totally to preclude any contact between black and white, especially when that contact was so sedulously proscribed by law.

Yet if white Southerners cannot "know" the Negro, it is for this very reason that the entire sexual myth needs to be re-examined. Surely a certain amount of sexual tension between the races does continue to exist, and the Southern white man's fear of sexual agression on the part of the Negro male is still too evident to be ignored. But the nature of the growth of the urban, modern South has been such as to impose ever more effective walls between the races. While it cannot be denied that slavery times produced an enormous amount of interbreeding (with all of its totalitarianism, this was a free-for-all atmosphere far less self-conscious about carnal mingling than the Jim Crow era which began in the 1890s) and while even now there must logically take place occasional sexual contacts between the races—especially in rural areas where a degree of casual familiarity has always obtained—the monolithic nature of segregation has raised such an effective barrier between whites and Negroes that it is impossible not to believe that theories involving a perpetual sexual "tension" have been badly inflated. Nor is it possible to feel that a desire to taste forbidden fruit has ever really caused this barrier to be breached. From the standpoint of the Negro, there is indifference or uncomplicated fear; from that of the white—segregation, the law, and, finally, indifference, too. When I was growing up, the older boys might crack wan jokes about visiting the Negro whorehouse street (patronized entirely, I later discovered, by Negroes plus a few Scandinavian sailors), but to my knowledge none of them ever really went there. Like Negroes in general, Negro girls were to white men phantoms, shadows. To assume that anything more than a rare and sporadic intimacy on any level has existed in the modern South between whites and Negroes is simply to deny, with a truly willful contempt for logic, the monstrous effectiveness of that apartheid which has been the Southern way of life for almost three-quarters of a century.

I have lingered on this matter only to try to underline a truth about Southern life which has been too often taken for granted, and which has therefore been overlooked or misinterpreted. Most Southern white people *cannot* know or touch black people and this is because of the deadly intimidation of a universal law. Certainly one feels the presence of this gulf even in the work of a writer as supremely knowledgeable about the South as William Faulkner, who confessed a hesitancy about attempting to "think Negro," and whose Negro characters, as marvelously portrayed as most of them are, seem nevertheless to be meticulously *observed* rather than *lived*. Thus in *The Sound and the Fury*, Faulkner's magnificent Dilsey comes richly alive, yet in retrospect one feels this is a result of countless mornings, hours, days Faulkner had spent watching and listening to old Negro servants, and not because Dilsey herself is a being created from a sense of withinness: at the last moment Faulkner draws back, and it is no mere happenstance that Dilsey, alone among the four central figures from whose points of view the story is told, is seen from the outside rather than from that intensely "inner" vantage point, the interior monologue.

Innumerable white Southerners have grown up as free of knowledge of the Negro character and soul as a person whose background is rural Wisconsin or Maine. Yet, of course, there is a difference, and it is a profound one, defining the white Southerner's attitudes and causing him to be, for better or for worse, whatever it is he is to be. For the Negro is *there*. And he is there in a way he never is in the North, no matter how great his numbers. In the South he is a perpetual and immutable part of history itself, a piece of the vast fabric so integral and necessary that without him the fabric dissolves; his voice, his black or brown face passing on a city street, the sound of his cry rising from a wagonload of flowers, his numberless procession down dusty country roads, the neat white church he has built in some pine grove with its air of grace and benison and tranquillity, his silhouette behind a mule team far off in some spring field, the wail of his blues blaring from some jukebox in a backwoods roadhouse, the sad wet faces of nursemaids and cooks waiting in the evening at city bus stops in pouring rain—the Negro is always *there*.

No wonder then, as Ellison says, the white Southerner can do virtually nothing without responding to the presence of Negroes. No wonder the white man so often grows cranky, fanciful, freakish, loony, violent: how else respond to a paradox which requires, with the full majesty of law behind it, that he deny the very reality of a people whose multitude approaches and often exceeds his own; that he disclaim the existence of those whose human presence has marked every acre of the land, every hamlet and crossroad and city and town, and whose humanity, however inflexibly denied, is daily evidenced to him like a heartbeat in loyalty and wickedness, madness and hilarity and mayhem and pride and love? The Negro may feel that it is too late to be known, and that the desire to know him reeks of outrageous condescension. But to break down the old law, to come to *know* the Negro, has become the moral imperative of every white Southerner.

I I

I suspect that my search for Nat Turner, my own private attempt as a novelist to re-create and bring alive that dim and prodigious black man, has been at least a partial fulfillment of this mandate, although the problem has long since resolved itself into an artistic one—which is as it should be. In the late 1940s, having finished college in North Carolina and come to New York, I found myself again haunted by that name I had first seen in the Virginia history textbook. I had learned something more of Southern history since then, and I had become fascinated by the subject of Negro slavery. One of the most striking aspects of the institution is the fact that in the 250 years of its existence in America, it was singularly free of organized uprisings, plots, and rebellions. (It is curious that as recently as the late 1940s, scholarly insights were lagging, and I could only have suspected then what has since been made convincing by such historians as Frank Tannenbaum and Stanley Elkins: that American Negro slavery, unique in its psychological oppressiveness—the worst the world has ever known—was simply so despotic and emasculating as to render organized revolt next to impossible.) There were three exceptions: a conspiracy by the slave Gabriel Prosser and his followers near Richmond in the year 1800, the plot betrayed, the conspirators hanged; a similar conspiracy in 1822, in Charleston, South Carolina, led by a free Negro named Denmark Vesey, who also was betrayed before he could carry out his plans, and who was executed along with other members of the plot.

The last exception, of course, was Nat Turner, and he alone in the entire annals of American slavery—alone among all those "many thousand gone"—achieved a kind of triumph.

Even today, many otherwise well-informed people have never heard the name Nat Turner, and there are several plausible reasons for such an ignorance. One of these, of course, is that the study of our history—and not alone in the South—has been tendentious in the extreme, and has often avoided even an allusion to a figure like Nat, who inconveniently disturbs our notion of a slave system which, though morally wrong, was conducted with such charity and restraint that any organized act of insurrectory and murderous violence would be unthinkable. But a general ignorance about Nat Turner is even more understandable in view of the fact that so little is left of the actual record. Southampton County, which even now is off the beaten track, was at that period the remotest backwater imaginable. The relativity of time allows us elastic definitions: 1831 was yesterday. Yet the year 1831, in the Presidency of Andrew Jackson, lay in the very dawn of our modern history, three years before a railroad ever touched the soil of Virginia, a full fifteen years before the use of the telegraph. The rebellion itself was of such a cataclysmic nature as practically to guarantee confusion of the news, distortion, wild rumors, lies, and, finally, great areas of darkness and suppression; all of these have contributed to Nat's obscurity.

As for the contemporary documents themselves, only one survives: the *Confessions of Nat Turner*, a brief pamphlet of some five thousand words, transcribed from Nat's lips as he awaited trial, by a somewhat enigmatic lawyer named Thomas Gray, who published the *Confessions* in Baltimore and then vanished from sight. There are several discrepancies in Gray's transcript but it was taken down in haste, and in all major respects it seems completely honest and reliable. Those few newspaper accounts of the time, from Richmond and Norfolk, are sketchy, remote, filled with conjecture, and are thus virtually worthless. The existing county court records of Southampton remain brief and unilluminating, dull lists, a dry catalogue of names in fading ink: the white people slain, the Negroes tried and transported south, or acquitted, or convicted and hanged.

Roughly seventy years after the rebellion (in 1900, which by coincidence was the year Virginia formally adopted its first Jim Crow laws), the single scholarly book ever to be written on the affair was published—*The Southampton Insurrection*, by a Johns Hopkins Ph.D. candidate named William S. Drewry, who was an unreconstructed Virginian of decidedly pro-slavery leanings and a man so quaintly committed to the *ancien régime* that, in the midst of a description of the ghastliest part of the uprising, he was able to reflect that "slavery in Virginia was not such to arouse rebellion, but was an institution which nourished the strongest affection and piety in slave and owner, as well as moral qualities worthy of any age of civilization." For Drewry, Nat Turner was some sort of inexplicable aberration, like a man from Mars. Drewry was close enough to the event in time, however, to be able to interview quite a few of the survivors, and since he also possessed a bloodthirsty relish for detail, it was possible for him to reconstruct the chronology of the insurrection with what appears to be considerable accuracy. Drewry's book (it is of course long out of print) and Nat's *Confessions* remain the only significant sources about the insurrection. Of Nat himself, his background and early years, very little can be known. This is not disadvantageous to a novelist, since it allows him to speculate—with a freedom not accorded the historian—upon all the intermingled miseries, ambitions, frustrations, hopes, rages, and desires which caused this extraordinary black man to rise up out of those early mists of our history and strike down his oppressors with a fury of retribution unequaled before or since.

He was born in 1800, which would have made him at the time of the insurrection thirty-one years old—exactly the age of so many great revolutionaries at the decisive moment of their insurgency: Martin Luther,* Robespierre, Danton, Fidel Castro. Thomas Gray, in a footnote to the *Confessions,* describes him as having the "true Negro face" (an offhand way of forestalling an assumption that he might have possessed any white blood), and he adds that "for natural intelligence and quickness of apprehension he is surpassed by few men I have ever seen"—a lofty tribute indeed at that inflammatory instant, with antebellum racism at its most hysteric pitch. Although little is known for certain of Nat's childhood and youth, there can be no doubt that he was very precocious and that he learned not only to read and write with ease—an illustrious achievement in itself,

---

* See Erik Erikson's *Young Man Luther* (New York, W. W. Norton & Co., Inc., 1958) for a brilliant study of the development of the revolutionary impulse in a young man, and the relationship of this impulse to the father-figure. Although it is best to be wary of any heavy psychoanalytical emphasis, one cannot help believing that Nat Turner's relationship with his father, like Luther's, was tormented and complicated, especially since this person could not have been his real father, who ran away when Nat was an infant, but the white man who owned and raised him.

when learning to read and write was forbidden to Negroes by law—but at an early age acquired a knowledge of astronomy, and later on experimented in making paper and gunpowder. (The resemblance here to the knowledge of the ancient Chinese is almost too odd to be true, but I can find no reason to doubt it.)

The early decades of the nineteenth century were years of declining prosperity for the Virginia Tidewater, largely because of the ruination of the land through greedy cultivation of tobacco—a crop which had gradually disappeared from the region, causing the breakup of many of the big old plantations and the development of subsistence farming on small holdings. It was in these surroundings —a flat pastoral land of modest farms and even more modest homesteads, where it was rare to find a white man prosperous enough to own more than half a dozen Negroes, and where two or three slaves to a family was the general rule—that Nat was born and brought up, and in these surroundings he prepared himself for the apocalyptic role he was to play in history. Because of the failing economic conditions, it was not remarkable that Nat was purchased and sold several times by various owners (in a sense, he was fortunate in not having been sold off to the deadly cotton and rice plantations of South Carolina and Georgia, which was the lot of many Virginia Negroes of the period); and although we do not know much about any of these masters, the evidence does not appear to be that Nat was ill-treated, and in fact one of these owners (Samuel Turner, brother of the man on whose property Nat was born) developed so strong a paternal feeling for the boy and such regard for Nat's abilities, that he took the fateful step of encouraging him in the beginnings of an education.

The atmosphere of the time and place was fundamentalist and devout to a passionate degree, and at some time during his twenties Nat, who had always been a godly person—"never owning a dollar, never uttering an oath, never drinking intoxicating liquors, and never committing a theft"—became a Baptist preacher. Compared to the Deep South, Virginia slave life was not so rigorous; Nat must have been given considerable latitude, and found many opportunities to preach and exhort the Negroes. His gifts for preaching, for prophecy, and his own magnetism seem to have been so extraordinary that he grew into a rather celebrated figure among the Negroes of the county, his influence even extending to the whites, one of whom—a poor, half-cracked, but respectable overseer named Brantley—he converted to the faith and baptized in a mill pond in the sight of a multitude of the curious, both black and white. (After this no one would have anything to do with Brantley, and he left the county in disgrace.)

At about this time Nat began to withdraw into himself, fasting and praying, spending long hours in the woods or in the swamp, where he communed with the Spirit and where there came over him, urgently now, intimations that he was being prepared for some great purpose. His fanaticism grew in intensity, and during these lonely vigils in the forest he began to see apparitions:

I saw white spirits and black spirits engaged in battle, and the sun was darkened; the thunder rolled in the heavens and blood flowed in streams. . . . I wondered greatly at these miracles, and prayed to be informed of a certainty of the meaning thereof; and shortly afterwards, while laboring in the fields, I discovered drops of blood on the corn as though it were dew from heaven. For as the blood of Christ had been shed on this earth, and had ascended to heaven for the salvation of sinners, it was now returning to earth again in the form of dew. . . . On the twelfth day of May, 1828, I heard a loud noise in the heavens, and the Spirit instantly appeared to me and said the Serpent was loosened, and Christ had laid down the yoke he had borne for the sins of men, and that I should take it on and fight against the Serpent, for the time was fast approaching when the first should be last and the last should be first. . . .

Like all revolutions, that of Nat Turner underwent many worrisome hesitations, false starts, procrastinations, delays (with appropriate irony, Independence Day, 1830, had been one of the original dates selected, but Nat fell sick and the moment was put off again); finally, however, on the night of Sunday, August 21, 1831, Nat, together with five other Negroes in whom he had placed his confidence and trust, assembled in the woods near the home of his owner of the time, a carriage maker named Joseph Travis, and commenced to carry out a plan of total annihilation. The penultimate goal was the capture of the county seat, then called Jerusalem (a connotation certainly not lost on Nat, who, with the words of the prophets roaring in his ears, must have felt like Gideon himself before the extermination of the Midianites); there were guns and ammunition in Jerusalem, and with these captured it was then Nat's purpose to sweep thirty miles eastward, gathering black recruits on the way until the Great Dismal Swamp was reached—a snake-filled and gloomy fastness in which Nat believed, with probable justification, only Negroes could survive, and no white man's army could penetrate. The immediate objective, however, was the destruction of every white man, woman, and child on the ten-mile route to Jerusalem; no one was to be spared; tender infancy and feeble old age alike were to perish by the axe and the sword. The command, of course, was that of God Almighty, through the voice of his prophet Ezekiel: *Son of Man, prophesy and say, Thus saith the Lord; Say, a sword, a sword is sharpened, and also furbished: it is sharpened to make a sore slaughter.... Slay utterly old and young, both maids and little children, and women....* It was a scheme so wild and daring that it could only have been the product of the most wretched desperation and frustrate misery of soul; and of course it was doomed to catastrophe not only for whites but for Negroes—and for black men in ways which from the vantage point of history now seem almost unthinkable.

They did their job rapidly and with merciless and methodical determination. Beginning at the home of Travis—where five people, including a six-month-old infant, were slain in their beds—they marched from house to house on an eastward route, pillaging, murdering, sparing no one. Lacking guns—at least to begin with—they employed axes, hatchets, and swords as their tools of destruction, and swift decapitation was their usual method of dispatch. (It is interesting that the Negroes did not resort to torture, nor were they ever accused of rape. Nat's attitude toward sex was Christian and high-minded, and he had said: "We will not do to their women what they have done to ours.")

On through the first day they marched, across the hot August fields, gaining guns and ammunition, horses, and a number of willing recruits. That the insurrection was not purely racial, but perhaps obscurely pre-Marxist, may be seen in the fact that a number of dwellings belonging to poor white people were pointedly passed by. At midday on Monday their force had more than tripled, to the amount of nineteen, and nearly thirty white people lay dead. By this time, the alarm had been sounded throughout the country, and while the momentum of the insurgent band was considerable, many of the whites had fled in panic to the woods, and some of the farmers had begun to resist, setting up barricades from which they could fire back at Nat's forces. Furthermore, quite a few of the rebels had broken into the brandy cellars of the houses they had attacked and had gotten roaring drunk—an eventuality Nat had feared and had warned against. Nevertheless, the Negroes—augmented now by forty more volunteers—pressed on toward Jerusalem, continuing the attack into the next night and all through the following day, when at last obstinate resistance by the aroused whites and the appearance of a mounted force of militia troops (also, it must be suspected, continued attrition by the apple brandy) caused the rebels to be dispersed, only a mile or so from Jerusalem.

Almost every one of the Negroes was rounded up and brought to trial—a legalistic nicety characteristic of a time in which it was necessary for one to determine whether *his* slave, property, after all, worth eight or nine hundred dollars, was really guilty and deserving of the gallows. Nat disappeared immediately after the insurrection, and hid in the woods for over two months, when near-starvation and the onset of autumnal cold drove him from his cave and forced him to surrender to a lone farmer with a shotgun. Then he too was brought to trial in Jerusalem—early in November 1831—for fomenting a rebellion in which sixty white people had perished.

The immediate consequences of the insurrection were exceedingly grim. The killing of so many white people was in itself an act of futility. It has never been determined with any accuracy how many black people, not connected with the rebellion, were slain at the hands of rampaging bands of white men who swarmed all over Southampton in the week following the uprising, seeking reprisal and vengeance. A contemporary estimate by a Richmond newspaper, which deplored this retaliation, put the number at close to two hundred Negroes, many of them free, and many of them tortured in ways unimaginably horrible. But even more important was the effect that Nat Turner's insurrection had upon the institution of slavery at large. News of the revolt spread among Southern whites with great speed: the impossible, the unspeakable had at last taken place after two hundred years of the ministrations of sweet old mammies and softly murmured Yassuhs and docile compliance—and a shock wave of anguish and terror ran through the entire South. If such a nightmarish calamity happened there, would it not happen *here?*—here in Tennessee, in Augusta, in Vicksburg, in these bayous of Louisiana? Had Nat lived to see the consequences of his rebellion, surely it would have been for him the cruelest irony that his bold and desperate bid for liberty had caused only the most tyrannical new controls to be imposed upon Negroes everywhere—the establishment of patrols, further restrictions upon movement, education, assembly, and the beginning of other severe and crippling restraints which persisted throughout the slaveholding states until the Civil War. Virginia had been edging close to emancipation, and it seems reasonable to believe that the example of Nat's rebellion, stampeding many moderates in the legislature into a conviction that the Negroes could not be safely freed, was a decisive factor in the ultimate victory of the proslavery forces. Had Virginia, with its enormous prestige among the states, emancipated its slaves, the effect upon our history would be awesome to contemplate.

Nat brought cold, paralyzing fear to the South, a fear that never departed. If white men had sown the wind with chattel slavery, in Nat Turner they had reaped the whirlwind for white and black alike.

Nat was executed, along with sixteen other Negroes who had figured large in the insurrection. Most of the others were transported south, to the steaming fields of rice and cotton. On November 11, 1831, Nat was hanged from a live oak tree in the town square of Jerusalem. He went to his death with great dignity and courage. "The bodies of those executed," wrote Drewry, "with one exception, were buried in a decent and becoming manner. That of Nat Turner was delivered to the doctors, who skinned it and made grease of the flesh."

III

Not long ago, in the spring of the year, when I was visiting my family in Virginia, I decided to go down for the day to Southampton County, which is a drive of an hour and a half by car from the town where I was born and raised. Nat Turner was of course the reason for this trip, although I had nothing particular or urgent in mind. What research it was possible to do on the event I had long since done. The Southampton court records, I had already been reliably informed, would prove unrewarding. It was not a question, then, of digging out more facts, but simply a matter of wanting to savor the mood and atmosphere of a landscape I had not seen for quite a few years, since the times when as a boy I used to pass through Southampton on the way to my father's family home in North Carolina. I thought also that there might be a chance of visiting some of the historic sites connected with the insurrection, and perhaps even of retracing part of the route of the uprising through the help of one of those handsomely produced guidebooks for which the Historical Commission of Virginia is famous—guides indispensable for a trip to such Old Dominion shrines as Jamestown and Appomattox and Monticello. I became even more eager to go when one of my in-laws put me in touch by telephone with a cousin of his. This man, whom I shall call Dan Seward, lived near Franklin, the main town of Southampton, and he assured me in those broad cheery Southern tones which are like a warm embrace—and which, after long years in the chill North, are to me always so familiar, reminiscent, and therefore so unsettling, sweet, and curiously painful—that he would like nothing better than to aid me in my exploration in whatever way he could.

Dan Seward is a farmer, and prosperous grower of peanuts in a prosperous agricultural region where the peanut is the unquestioned monarch. A combination of sandy loam soil and a long growing season has made Southampton ideal for the cultivation of peanuts; over 30,000 acres are planted annually, and the crop is processed and marketed in Franklin—a thriving little town of 7,000 people— or in Suffolk and Portsmouth, where it is rendered into Planters cooking oil and stock feed and Skippy peanut butter. There are other money-making crops—corn and soybeans and cotton. The county is at the northernmost edge of the cotton belt, and thirty years ago cotton was a major source of income. Cotton has declined in importance but the average yield per acre is still among the highest in the South, and the single gin left in the county in the little village of Drewryville processes each year several thousand bales which are trucked to market down in North Carolina. Lumbering is also very profitable, owing mainly to an abundance of the loblolly pines valuable in the production of kraft wood pulp; and the Union Bag-Camp Paper Company's plant on the Blackwater river in Franklin is a huge enterprise employing over 1,600 people. But it is peanuts—the harvested vines in autumn piled up mile after mile in dumpy brown stacks like hay—which have brought money to Southampton, and a sheen of prosperity that can be seen in the freshly painted farmhouses along the monotonously flat state highway which leads into Franklin, and the new-model Dodges and Buicks parked slantwise against the curb of some crossroads hamlet, and the gaudy, eye-catching signs that advise the wisdom of a bank savings account for all those surplus funds.

The county has very much the look of the New South about it, with its airport and its shiny new motels, its insistent billboards advertising space for industrial sites, the sprinkling of housing developments with television antennas gleaming from every rooftop, its supermarkets and shopping centers and its flavor of go-getting commercialism. This is the New South, where agriculture still prevails but has joined in a vigorous union with industry, so that even the peanut when it goes to market is ground up in some rumbling engine of commerce and becomes metamorphosed into wood stain or soap or cattle feed. The Negroes, too, have partaken of this abundance—some of it, at least—for they own television sets also, and if not new-model Buicks (the Southern white man's strictures against Negro ostentation remain intimidating), then decent late-model used Fords; while in the streets of Franklin the Negro women shopping seemed on the day of my visit very proud and well-dressed compared to the shabby stooped figures I recalled from the Depression years when I was a boy. It would certainly appear that Negroes deserve some of this abundance, if only because they make up so large a part of the work force. Since Nat Turner's day the balance of population in Southampton—almost 60 per cent Negro—has hardly altered by a hair.

"I don't know anywhere that a Negro is treated better than around here," Mr. Seward was saying to the three of us, on the spring morning I visited him with my wife and my father. "You take your average person from up North, he just doesn't *know* the Negro like we do. Now for instance I have a Negro who's worked for me for years, name of Ernest. He knows if he breaks his arm—like he did a while ago, fell off a tractor—he knows he can come to me and I'll see that he's taken care of, hospital expenses and all, and I'll take care of him and his family while he's unable to work, right on down the line. I don't ask him to pay back a cent, either, that's for sure. We have a wonderful relationship, that Negro and myself. By God, I'd die for that Negro and he knows it, and he'd do the same for me. But Ernest doesn't want to sit down at my table, here in this house, and have supper with me—and he wouldn't want me in *his* house. And Ernest's got kids like I do, and he doesn't want them to go to school with my Bobby, any more than Bobby wants to go to school with *his* kids. It works both ways. People up North don't seem to be able to understand a simple fact like that."

Mr. Seward was a solidly fleshed, somewhat rangy, big-shouldered man in his early forties with an open, cheerful manner which surely did nothing to betray the friendliness with which he had spoken on the telephone. He had greeted us—total strangers, really—with an animation and uncomplicated good will that would have shamed an Eskimo; and for a moment I realized that, after years amid the granite outcroppings of New England, I had forgotten that this *was* the passionate, generous, outgoing nature of the South, no artificial display but a social gesture as natural as breathing.

Mr. Seward had just finished rebuilding his farmhouse on the outskirts of town, and he had shown us around with a pride I found understandable: there was a sparkling electric kitchen worthy of an advertisement in *Life* magazine, some handsome modern furniture, and several downstairs rooms paneled beautifully in the prodigal and lustrous hardwood of the region. It was altogether a fine, tasteful house, resembling more one of the prettier medium-priced homes in the Long Island suburbs than the house one might contemplate for a Tidewater farmer. Upstairs, we had inspected his son Bobby's room, a kid's room with books like *Pinocchio* and *The Black Arrow* and *The Swiss Family Robinson,* and here there was a huge paper banner spread across one entire wall with the crayon inscription: "Two . . . four . . . six . . . eight . . . We Don't Want to Integrate!" It was a sign which so overwhelmingly dominated the room that it could not help provoking comment, and it was this that eventually had led to Mr. Seward's reflections about *knowing* Negroes.

There might have been something vaguely defensive in his remarks but not a trace of hostility. His tone was matter-of-fact and good-natured, and he pronounced the word Negro as "nigra," which most Southerners do with utter naturalness while intending no disrespect whatsoever, in fact quite the opposite—the mean epithet, of course, is "nigger." I had the feeling that Mr. Seward had begun amiably to regard us as sympathetic but ill-informed outsiders, non-Southern, despite his knowledge of my Tidewater background and my father's own accent, which is thick as grits. Moreover, the fact that I had admitted to having lived in the North for fifteen years caused me, I fear, to appear alien in his eyes, *déraciné*, especially when my acculturation to Northern ways has made me adopt the long "e" and say Negro. The racial misery, at any rate, is within inches of driving us mad: how can I explain that, with all my silent disagreement with Mr. Seward's paternalism, I knew that when he said, "By God, I'd die for that Negro," he meant it?

Perhaps I should not have been surprised that Mr. Seward seemed to know very little about Nat Turner. When we got around to the subject, it developed that he had always thought that the insurrection occurred way back in the eighteenth century. Affably, he described seeing in his boyhood the "Hanging Tree," the live oak from which Nat had been executed in Courtland (Jerusalem had undergone this change of name after the Civil War), and which had died and been cut down some thirty years ago; as for any other landmarks, he regretted that he did not know of a single one. No, so far as he knew, there just wasn't anything.

For me, it was the beginning of disappointments which grew with every hour. Had I *really* been so ingenuous as to believe that I would unearth some shrine, some home preserved after the manner of Colonial Williamsburg, a relic of the insurrection at whose portal I would discover a lady in billowing satin and crinoline, who for fifty cents would shepherd me about the rooms with a gentle drawl indicating the spot where a good mistress fell at the hands of the murderous darky? The native Virginian, despite himself, is cursed with a suffocating sense of history, and I do not think it impossible that I actually suspected some such monument. Nevertheless, confident that there would be something to look at, I took heart when Mr. Seward suggested that after lunch we all drive over to Courtland, ten miles to the west. He had already spoken to a friend of his, the Sheriff of the county, who knew all the obscure byways and odd corners of Southampton, mainly because of his endless search for illegal stills; if there was a solitary person alive who might be able to locate some landmark, or could help retrace part of Nat Turner's march, it was the Sheriff. This gave me hope. For I had brought along Drewry's book and its map which showed the general route of the uprising, marking the houses by name. In the sixty years since Drewry, there would have been many changes in the landscape. But with this map oriented against the Sheriff's detailed county map, I should easily be able to pick up the trail and thus experience, however briefly, a sense of the light and shadow that played over that scene of slaughter and retribution a hundred and thirty-four years ago.

Yet it was as if Nat Turner had never existed, and as the day lengthened and afternoon wore on, and as we searched Nat's part of the county—five of us now, riding in the Sheriff's car with its huge star emblazoned on the doors, and its radio blatting out hoarse intermittent messages, and its riot gun protectively nuzzling the backs of our necks over the edge of the rear seat—I had the sensation from time to time that this Negro, who had so long occupied my thoughts, who indeed had so obsessed my imagination that he had acquired larger spirit and flesh than most of the living people I encountered day in and day out, had been merely a crazy figment of my mind, a phantom no more real than some half-recollected image from a fairy tale. For here in the back country, this horizontal land of woods and meadows where he had roamed, only a few people had heard of Nat Turner, and of those who had—among the people we stopped to make inquiries of, both white and black, along dusty country roads, at farms, at filling stations, at crossroad stores—most of them confused him, I think, with something spectral, mythic, a black Paul Bunyan who had perpetrated mysterious and nameless deeds in millennia past. They were neither facetious nor evasive, simply unaware. Others confounded him with the Civil War—a Negro general. One young Negro field hand, lounging at an Esso station, figured he was a white man. A white man, heavy-lidded and paunchy, slow-witted, an idler at a rickety store, thought him an illustrious race-horse of bygone days.

The Sheriff, a smallish, soft-speaking ruminative man, with the whisper of a smile frozen on his face as if he were perpetually enjoying a good joke, knew full well who Nat Turner was, and I could tell he relished our frustrating charade. He was a shrewd person, quick and sharp with countrified wisdom, and he soon became quite as fascinated as I with the idea of tracking down some relic of the uprising (although he said that Drewry's map was hopelessly out of date, the roads of that time now abandoned to the fields and woods, the homes burnt down or gone to ruin); the country people's ignorance he found irresistible and I think it tickled him to perplex their foolish heads, white or black, with the same old leading question: "You heard about old Nat Turner, ain't you?" But few of them had heard, even though I was sure that many had plowed the same fields that Nat had crossed, lived on land that he had passed by; and as for dwellings still standing which might have been connected with the rebellion, not one of these back-country people could offer the faintest hint or clue. As effectively as a monstrous and unbearable dream, Nat had been erased from memory.

It was late afternoon when, with a sense of deep fatigue and frustration, I suggested to Mr. Seward and the Sheriff that maybe we had better go back to Courtland and call it a day. They were agreeable—relieved, I felt, to be freed of this tedious and fruitless search—and as we headed east down a straight unpaved road, the conversation became desultory, general. We spoke of the North. The Sheriff was interested to learn that I often traveled to New York. He went there occasionally himself, he said; indeed, he had been there only the month before—"to pick up a nigger," a fugitive from custody who had been awaiting trial for killing his wife. New York was a fine place to spend the night, said the Sheriff, but he wouldn't want to live there.

As he spoke, I had been gazing out of the window, and now suddenly something caught my eye—something familiar, a brief flickering passage of a distant outline, a silhouette against the sun-splashed woods—and I asked the Sheriff to stop the car. He did, and as we backed up slowly through a cloud of dust, I recognized a house standing perhaps a quarter of a mile off the road, from this distance only a lopsided oblong sheltered by an enormous oak, but the whole tableau—the house and the glorious hovering tree and the stretch of woods beyond—so familiar to me that it might have been some home I passed every day. And of course now as recognition came flooding back, I knew whose house it was. For in *The Southampton Insurrection*, the indefatigable Drewry had included many photographs—amateurish, doubtless taken by himself, and suffering from the fuzzy offset reproduction of 1900. But they were clear enough to provide an unmistakable guide to the dwellings in question, and now as I again consulted the book I could see that this house—the monumental oak above it grown scant inches it seemed in sixty years—was the one referred to by Drewry as having belonged to Mrs. Catherine Whitehead. From this distance, in the soft clear light of a spring afternoon, it seemed most tranquil, but few houses have come to know such a multitude of violent deaths. There in the late afternoon of Monday, August 22, Nat Turner and his band had appeared, and they set upon and killed "Mrs. Catherine Whitehead, son Richard, and four daughters, and grandchild."

The approach to the house was by a rutted lane long ago abandoned and overgrown with lush weeds which made a soft, crushed, rasping sound as we rolled over them. Dogwood, white and pink, grew on either side of the lane, quite wild and wanton in lovely pastel splashes. Not far from the house a pole fence interrupted our way; the Sheriff stopped the car and we got out and stood there for a moment, looking at the place. It was quiet and still—so quiet that the sudden chant of a mockingbird in the woods was almost frightening —and we realized then that no one lived in the house. Scoured by weather, paintless, worn down to the wintry gray of bone and with all the old mortar gone from between the timbers, it stood alone and desolate above its blasted, sagging front porch, the ancient door ajar like an open wound. Although never a manor house, it had once been a spacious and comfortable country home; now in near-ruin it sagged, finished, a shell, possessing only the most fragile profile of itself. As we drew closer still we could see that the entire house, from its upper story to the cellar, was filled with thousands of shucked ears of corn—feed for the malevolent-looking little razorback pigs which suddenly appeared in a tribe at the edge of the house, eying us, grunting. Mr. Seward sent them scampering with a shied stick and a farmer's sharp "Whoo!" I looked up at the house, trying to recollect its particular role in Nat's destiny, and then I remembered.

There was something baffling, secret, irrational about Nat's own participation in the uprising. He was unable to kill. Time and time again in his confession one discovers him saying (in an offhand tone; one must dig for the implications): "I could not give the death blow, the hatchet glanced from his head," or, "I struck her several blows over the head, but I was unable to kill her, as the sword was dull. . . ." It is too much to believe, over and over again: the glancing hatchet, the dull sword. It smacks rather, as in *Hamlet*, of rationalization, ghastly fear, an access of guilt, a shrinking from violence, and fatal irresolution. Alone here at this house, turned now into a huge corncrib around which pigs rooted and snorted in the silence of a spring afternoon, here alone was Nat finally able—or was he forced?—to commit a murder, and this upon a girl of eighteen named Margaret Whitehead, described by Drewry in terms perhaps not so romantic or farfetched after all, as "the belle of the county." The scene is apocalyptic—afternoon bedlam in wild harsh sunlight and August heat.

"I returned to commence the work of death, but those whom I left had not been idle; all the family were already murdered but Mrs. Whitehead and her daughter Margaret. As I came round the door I saw Will pulling Mrs. Whitehead out of the house and at the step he nearly severed her head from her body with his axe. Miss Margaret, when I discovered her, had concealed herself in the corner formed by the projection of the cellar cap from the house; on my approach she fled into the field but was soon overtaken and after repeated blows with a sword, I killed her by a blow on the head with a fence rail."

It is Nat's only murder. Why, from this point on, does the momentum of the uprising diminish, the drive and tension sag? Why, from this moment in the *Confessions*, does one sense in Nat something dispirited, listless, as if all life and juice had been drained from him, so that never again through the course of the rebellion is he even on the scene when a murder is committed? What happened to Nat in this place? Did he discover his humanity here, or did he lose it?

I lifted myself up into the house, clambering through a doorway without steps, pushing myself over the crumbling sill. The house had a faint yeasty fragrance, like flat beer. Dust from the mountains of corn lay everywhere in the deserted rooms, years and decades of dust, dust an inch thick in some places, lying in a fine gray powder like sooty fallen snow. Off in some room amid the piles of corn I could hear a delicate scrabbling and a plaintive squeaking of mice. Again it was very still, the shadow of the prodigious old oak casting a dark pattern of leaves, checkered with bright sunlight, aslant through the gaping door. As in those chilling lines of Emily Dickinson, even this lustrous and golden day seemed to find its only resonance in the memory, and perhaps a premonition, of death.

> This quiet Dust was Gentlemen and Ladies,
> And Lads and Girls;
> Was laughter and ability and sighing,
> And frocks and curls.

Outside, the Sheriff was calling in on his car radio, his voice blurred and indistinct; then the return call from the county seat, loud, a dozen incomprehensible words in an uproar of static. Suddenly it was quiet again, the only sound my father's soft voice as he chatted with Mr. Seward.

I leaned against the rotting frame of the door, gazing out past the great tree and into that far meadow where Nat had brought down and slain Miss Margaret Whitehead. For an instant, in the silence, I thought I could hear a mad rustle of taffeta, and rushing feet, and a shrill girlish piping of terror; then that day and this day seemed to meet and melt together, becoming almost one, and for a long moment indistinguishable.

III

The Impending Crisis
of the Deep South

♦

by D. W. Brogan

It is not from laziness that I have chosen to borrow the title of Hinton Rowan Helper's tract, the only rival to *Uncle Tom's Cabin* in the Southern *Index Expurgatorius* of the doom laden period just before the outbreak of "The War Between the States." For that the Deep South is in a crisis can hardly be doubted. Its traditional social order is being threatened from the outside and, rather covertly, from the inside, and it is being defended by methods that may be as revolutionary as any suggested by internal or external critics—and far more disastrous.

The crisis which we may, for convenience' sake, date from the desegregation decision of 1954 has been made suddenly even more acute by further court decisions—those that threaten rural political dominance, for instance—and by the political secession of five Southern states (South Carolina, Georgia, Alabama, Louisiana, Mississippi) from the Union in the 1964 elections. For the election results are novel and ominous. It is not merely that Georgia for the first time has voted Republican—and that Vermont for the first time has voted Democratic. It is that over a great part of the Deep South, effective rational political leadership has been defeated (where it existed); that what, in many ways, was a promising development, the rise of a two-party South, has been parodied; and that in a Gadarene rush the Deep South, the archaic South, has imitated, has, indeed, surpassed the follies of 1860 and 1861.

Of course, the political folly is only a symptom of a deeper refusal to accept or reject the modern world. Yet the political failure makes a convenient diving board for the rash speculator who wonders what has happened, what *can* happen to a region so blind to its economic and social realities as well as to its material interests. To "call a nettle but a nettle and the faults of fools but folly" is not really very helpful. We must understand, if we can, the why as well as the how of the parody of national politics as exemplified in the Deep South last November. We must try to comprehend the nature of "the impending crisis." We cannot understand if we do not continually tell ourselves: There but for the grace of God go I.

In addition to the general difficulties of the outsider, I am not only not a Southerner, I am not an American. I have no direct concern with the American "image," although as a citizen of a Western nation allied to the United States, I do have a great indirect interest. But being a foreigner, if it is a grave handicap, has some advantages. One is on the outside looking in; it is not that one sees deeper, but that one sees differently. The foreigner is less likely to erect temporary and accidental social arrangements into natural laws (as Croce said Aristotle did in *his* defense of slavery). He is more likely to see that much that is wrong with the South and that most embitters the critical minority (I am talking of the white minority; I know next to nothing about the Negro minority) is not peculiar to the South, can be paralleled from recent or indeed contemporary history, and is part of the price that has to be paid for belonging to "the so-called human race."

Shutting Out the World

Let us take, first of all, one of the primary obstacles to a rational entry of the Deep South into the modern technological world, in good order and with the preservation of the many things of repute that the region has and ought to preserve, the more that some of them are in short supply in the triumphant North, not to speak of censorious Europe. (I have in mind its genuine tradition of civility that has survived such defiances as the Bull Connors and the Jim Clarks and the Wallaces, some skepticism of the more foolish promises of the prophets of a technological paradise, some feeling for the tragic side of history which the North has not experienced and consequently does not realize it needs.) The obstacle is ignorance.

I am not trying to stress the fact that the South, partly because of poverty, is formally and, if you like, innocently ignorant, because of the defects of its institutional system. It was with astonishment that I read in Professor James Silver's admirable book, *Mississippi: The Closed Society*, that he *had* to write to a presumably literate citizen of the state that, "if you have the feeling that the University of Mississippi has any prominent position in the educational field at the present time, you are sadly misinformed." Yet Professor Silver knows far better than I what *is* believed in Mississippi about the academic status of Ole Miss. And the trouble is and has been, not the result of poverty only, but mainly the result of a desire to shut out completely the hostile, critical, or nonadmiring outside world.

Mississippi, or for that matter Alabama and the other Deep Southern states, are not alone in this desire. Verwoerd's South Africa cannot risk television or a critical Afrikaans university life. An absence of television may not be a great loss, but a mental state of siege is a very serious one. And it is not long since a very learned Irish Catholic, member of a famous Irish family, one who knows at first hand the universities of Ireland, told me of his sad conclusion that "you can't have a real university in a Catholic country." I think he was wrong, but you can't have a real university where such prelates as the present Archbishop of Dublin are criticized only in discreet speech or in foreign papers. And you can't have a real university where all is subordinated to the defense of one position, even if that position is highly defensible—and the Southern position is not. So I was not surprised to learn that many people in the Deep South really believed that Mr. Goldwater had a good chance of victory, that

Governor Wallace had actually made converts in the North, that *Brown v. Topeka* could be ignored or repealed, and that Appomattox had never happened.

Similar illusions, that the North wouldn't fight, that the Yankees were cowards, that "Cotton is King," were dearly paid for between 1861 and 1865. Yet Frank Owsley, a good critical historian when he wrote of the political incompetence of the Confederacy, blew his top when he contributed his hysterical article to the famous manifesto of 1930, *I'll Take My Stand.* It was a sign of the disastrous effects of the Southern siege mind that so distinguished a scholar could write of the leaders of the South before the War: "Their skirts were clear. Let the blood of slavery rest upon the heads of those who had forced it upon the South." Surely, Lincoln's acceptance of the guilt of North *and* South is both better history and better wisdom. But Owsley was on the defensive, *his* section needed an excuse for its defeat and it fell back, or was invited to fall back, on an heroic and maligned past and was warned against an odious and literally demoralizing future.

If we are to consider what holds the South back from the modern world in so graceless and often base a way, we must allow for the survival of the Confederate legend. This legend is now less an heroic memory than poison in the blood; it recalls less Chancellorsville, or even Nashville, than Oxford, Mississippi, with Ross Barnett as the poor man's Jefferson Davis. Of course, Southern pride in its military glory is natural, for it is all that the South salvaged in 1865. And the glory is genuine. Yet, politically, that cult of glory is one of the South's great handicaps today. The South did suffer, but in this bloody century so many nations have suffered more. Why should a citizen of Berlin or Rotterdam or, for that matter, London, listen with patience to the tale of the burning of Columbia or Atlanta or the fire at Charleston? It can become as tedious as Irish lamentations over "the Troubles." Should a world that has been witness of the siege of Leningrad waste much time on the qualified heroism of the defenders, military and civilian, of Vicksburg? Should the victims of Hitler and of the Red Army really be expected to stand the retelling of the crimes of Sherman? Should the survivors of Hiroshima be interrupted in their memories by what is now very ancient history?

Tragedy and Farce

If this military cult is excessive, it is at least based on a reality. But the political cult is based on a dangerous fiction. One of the most disastrous illusions of the antebellum South was that it was the home of statesmen; at best it was the home of rhetoricians and pedants. Did the antebellum South produce any seriously competent political leader after President Polk? It is very doubtful. I think it is true that Jefferson Davis was the best political leader the South could find, but what a commentary on the South that is! And Davis, we should remember, was not a fire-eater, not a forerunner of Wallace or Barnett—or of Goldwater. The South in 1861 showed more prudence in choosing leaders than it has been doing of late. It chose the best it had; they were not good enough. Even the saboteurs of the war effort, the fanatics of States' Rights—Brown of Georgia, Vance of North Carolina—were more respectable characters than the most vehement defenders of "the Southern Way of Life" today.

It is, and has been for a long time, the South—"Christian," "conservative," "constitutional," "Anglo-Saxon"—that has produced the buffoons, the liars, the merest demagogues, the adroit exploiters of the passions and ignorance of the ill-educated Southern voters. One may assume that a man who was a successful trial lawyer like Governor Barnett must know the folly of "interposition," and that a former president of the American Bar Association like Mr. John Satterfield must know more than he permits himself to say. But possibly Governor Paul Johnson of Mississippi and Governor Wallace of Alabama *do* believe the historical and legal nonsense they preach and, up to the point of danger, practice. They are the equivalents of the Barnwell Rhetts of the period before the War, of the rabid doctrinaires who made even Jefferson Davis have doubts about the political sagacity of his section.

But where are the leaders in the Deep South who *do* know better, who are at the intellectual level of President Lyndon Johnson of Texas? They are mostly silent or, when they give a lead, however discreetly, are disowned. South Carolina has preferred the lead of Senator Strom Thurmond to the lead of former Governor and now

Senator Donald Russell, as it preferred the lead of John C. Calhoun to the lead of James L. Petigru or Benjamin Franklin Perry. History, said Marx, *does* repeat itself; once as tragedy, then as farce.

But is is not only the present generations of leaders—and led—that have much to answer for. It is the survival of the bad tradition which made any adjustment between the victors and the vanquished impossible in 1865. It is in the nature of things that Mississippi was the leader in the rush of the conquered states to vote themselves victory by enacting the Black Codes. The South might have been better off if it had *really* been reconstructed, if the federal government had both imposed a new political pattern and given the equivalent of Marshall aid.

Not all the follies or sins were on one side. But many of the wrongs of Reconstruction, exaggerated and lied about as they were, were earned by the South. Folly has its price. To undo the "wrongs" inflicted by the Treaty of Versailles most Germans rallied behind Hitler and landed themselves in a political and moral disaster from which it is not at all certain that the German state will recover in this century. To undo the wrongs inflicted by the so-called victors in "the War of Northern Aggression," to borrow a phrase I picked up in Richmond a couple of years ago, the leaders of the South encouraged organized violence, organized lawlessness, organized mendacity. By these methods and by the aid of Northern moral laziness and greed, the South was "redeemed"—that is, a large part of the population of the South was by law, custom, education reduced to peonage, taught to see and comport themselves as "niggers," taught their place by physical outrage that has had its parallels in this dreadful century in the crimes of the Nazi SS, of the French "*milice*," of the Red Army, of the French "forces of order" in Algeria, and, as an earlier trial run, in British massacres in India and murderous and organized crime in Ireland. The South is not alone in its sins, but it is nearly alone in not admitting them to be sins.

You cannot organize a reign of terror for a generation, you cannot be silent when the Old Adam or Old Nick breaks out, without paying a price. The personal price does not matter, but the sectional price does. The sight of Senator James Eastland as chairman of the Senate

Judiciary Committee (by the grace of Northern Democratic votes) may strike some people as merely as scandalous as pious Catholics may have thought the sight of Alexander VI celebrating High Mass in St. Peter's. But it is symptomatic in an ugly sense. The necessary adjustment of the South to the modern world is hindered, possibly made impossible, by political phenomena like Senator Eastland. He matters; Senator Thurmond (Rep., S. C.) does not.

In what way does such a political incongruity matter in 1965? It matters because the adjustment to the modern world is not simply a question of getting modern industry—largely federal government industry—into the South. It is a matter of getting a climate of opinion in which the white people of Mississippi, of Alabama, of rural Georgia, can make the kind of revolutionary change in their public political attitudes that must be made if the Deep South is not to remain a sore and a scandal for the United States, a society that is getting sicker. It must get better or worse; it can't simply stew in its own juice.

It would be easy and tempting to let it go at that. We all like to "compound for sins [we] are inclined to by damning those [we] have no mind to." But it is not a mere matter of avoiding censoriousness, for we should first of all ask ourselves if, in fact, we *do* have no mind to? I recall one of the wisest sayings on the race question in the South, made thirty years ago by that acute observer and critic, Mr. Thomas Sancton. "Every white man is at heart a sahib." This is true of the South, and I am sure that Mr. Sancton meant it to be true of more than the South. He was right. The temptations of race superiority, of any conspicuous and accepted badge of superiority, like a "good accent" in England, are nearly irresistible. The intellect, the moral sense, may bid us reject them, but our wicked and corrupt hearts say "take them."

We have seen in England a safe Labor seat lost in Parliament on a "white backlash" vote of the kind that Governor Wallace failed to deliver in Gary, Indiana. I take it that Mr. Patrick Gordon Walker, the former Foreign Secretary who lost two safe seats, would be less inclined than most Labor MPs to be condescending about the race problems of the United States; and, of course, race is not the only prejudice. One reason for the slight Labor majority in England after the 1964 general elections was that certain districts of the Liverpool area at last went Labor because the descendants of Irish Protestants there no longer vote simply against the Pope. Labor would have had a more manageable majority if the Protestant voters of Ulster had voted their interests instead of their prejudices.

I could multiply the instances of nonracial prejudice that afflict advanced and complacent societies like Britain. But race is more powerful as a distorter of the democratic process. Race is visible; the race that is denied equality has known the greater inferiority of slavery. Its inheritance is ambiguous. The Negroes are Americans, but what *kind* of Americans? Are they complete Americans? The Southern tradition says No. Prejudice is there, is in some degree natural, is comfortable, and is, for some people, profitable. It may be that as Professor W. H. Hutt of Cape Town has ingeniously argued about South Africa, racial segregation is unprofitable, even a dead loss, to the segregators. But the South Africans don't know that, or the most noisy of them don't.

Ruling classes in all countries have been inclined for many centuries to encourage the lower orders to entertain dividing prejudices. Catholics in Ireland are kept from dangerous thoughts that might have awkward social consequences. The Tsardom encouraged or winked at pogroms. The best people in Germany professed to believe that they could use Hitler; that way Auschwitz lay. The Southern ruling class, the decaying planters, the rising businessmen, afraid, with faint reason I think, of an alliance of poor whites and blacks, until 1965 let the nigger-haters have their head.

This involved a lot of foolish and some odious nonsense. The history of Jim Crow, as C. Vann Woodward has pointed out, is nasty, brutish, and short. It produced such impudent absurdities as banning until 1959 the Atlanta public library to all Negroes, thus barring W. E. B. Du Bois, the most distinguished intellectual ornament of Atlanta. (I, although a fairly frequent visitor to Atlanta, didn't know Negroes were barred, and many intelligent Atlanta whites didn't know either. After all, it was no skin off our noses.) In Florida, there is a natural "wonder," the property of the state, a series of pools of exceptionally clear water over which you sail in glass-bottomed boats. Half of these boats are driven by Negroes, but no Negro can be a passenger—or could not be till quite recently. They *could,* however, go half a mile away and from the top of a lane look at their betters gliding over the water owned by the state of which they were citizens! Instances of such ignominious brutality could be multiplied. And they are not as serious as notorious inequalities in the administration of the law, the toleration of murder as an instrument of government in Mississippi, bad schools, economic inequality enhanced by law and custom; nor are they posssibly as serious as the congenital and sacred bad manners of some whites to Negroes. (Again, the sin is not purely Southern; if it is only now that a Negro in court is beginning to be called "Mister," it was a long time before Methodist ministers in England established the right to be called "Reverend.") It may be that the defense, to this day, of these absurd and degrading exclusions is part of what Messrs. Killian and Grigg in their highly intelligent book on the *Racial Crisis in America* call the "patriarchal" tradition, but patriarchal is an ambiguous term. The most hard-shell Baptist would not today hold up the patriarch Lot as a pattern.

But what has all this to do with the adjustment of the Deep South to modern society? I am not innocent enough to think that certain types of technical progress cannot be made in a society in which freedom, in our sense, is rare or unknown. The Sputniks were the product of an unfree society; so were Dr. Wernher von Braun's rockets. (I see no reason why Dr. von Braun should not work happily in Alabama; he has served a worse society with no known discomfort.) But American society is not quite like that of Stalin's Russia or Hitler's Germany. By far the great part of the intellectual leaders of America are committed to the "liberal" position. They do not feel at home in the Deep South. For that matter, intelligent Southerners do not feel at home there. They get out or are pushed out. Those who stay show heroic virtue.

That they go into exile or are exiled is a pity. But they run more than the risk of persecution if they stay; they run the risk of being infected by the local madness. I know a man, of a really aristocratic family, a Sartoris not a Snopes, who has been a scientific servant of the federal government, who has inherited wealth and made it much greater, who is above all economic pressure and socially far above a "new man" like Jefferson Davis, to name only the dead. Yet he is a sophisticated supporter of Governor Wallace. The politicians in Arkansas or Mississippi like Brooks Hays and Frank Smith who have shown what the Germans call "civil courage" have been duly punished. Even silence may not save Senators Sparkman or Hill of Alabama. His name may not, in a year or two, save Senator Long of Louisiana if madness still rules.

Salvation must come from the outside. It can come from men who have the decency to see the sins of their own side—as William Buckley displayed it in his reproach to the leaders of Mississippi who had not adequately denounced and punished the outrages against Negroes and Negro churches there. (Mr. Goldwater displayed a discreditable unwillingness to shoot the ducks that lay electoral eggs.) Most of the United States, indeed most of the South, has rebuked the follies—worse than follies—of the Goldwater campaign. It *is* an age in which anything, including some good things, may well seem possible. But if there should be no return to the spirit of Andrew Johnson's "treason must be made odious," there might be an amended version: treason must cease to be politically profitable.

"Children of Appomattox"

In a few years the United States may put a man on the moon. It will be an anomaly if it cannot effectively guarantee the rights of American citizens in Alabama and Mississippi, and if the Democratic party, which may by then be the only national party left, cannot dislodge a man like Senator Eastland. The Deep South can continue to try to secede inside the Union. The Union can prevent it if it wishes to; it can begin the political education too soon abandoned after history made sure that "the War Between the States" would be "the War of the Rebellion."

In an admirable speech on the hundred and fiftieth anniversary of the birth of Lincoln, Senator Lyndon Johnson, as he then was, said:

"We are all children of Appomattox." The choice must be made, between the spirit and achievement of Appomattox and the spirit of the proclamation of Jefferson Davis as President of the Confederacy, ominously, in Montgomery. Then it was said that the hour and the man had met. In a disastrous sense they had. The hour is here and a much more sagacious Southern leader is here. Will they meet?

IV

Georgia Boy Goes Home

♦

by Louis E. Lomax

I came home to Georgia by jet. The flight from New York to Atlanta
was uneventful, but as the plane taxied toward the terminal I felt
slightly uneasy. Georgia had just gone for Goldwater; Georgia was
still Georgia. Walking along the corridor to the main lobby, I heard
cracker twangs all about me; these, in my childhood, were the sound
of the enemy, so that even now I react when I hear them, and I
immediately suspect any white man who has a Southern drawl. Yet I
could see no signs telling me where I should eat, drink, or go to the
rest room. The white passengers seemed totally unconcerned with
me. I could see a change in their eyes, on their faces, in the way they
let me alone to be me.

I was on my way to the Southern Airlines counter to confirm my
reservation to Valdosta. Suddenly I saw a brown arm waving at me
from a phone booth. There, in the booth, was Martin Luther King,
Jr. Martin's family and mine had been Negro Baptist leaders in
Georgia for almost fifty years; I first got to know him when I was in
college and he was in junior high school. Now I was on my way
home to Valdosta for *Harper's* to write about the changes in my
town and to give a sermon in my uncle's church; Martin was on the
way to the island of Bimini to write his Nobel Prize acceptance
speech.

Martin and I stood in the lobby and tried to talk, but to no avail. We were continuously interrupted by white people who rushed over to shake his hand and pat him on the back. I could hardly believe that I was in Atlanta, that these were white people with twangs, and that they were saying what they were saying. Many of them asked for Martin's autograph; a few of them recognized me from television or from the dust jacket of a book and asked me to sign slips of paper. They were an incredible lot: a group of soldiers, five sailors, three marines, a score of civilians including the brother of the present Governor of Georgia, and three Negro girls. One stately old white man walked up to Martin and said, "By God, I don't like all you're doing, but as a fellow Georgian I'm proud of you."

My flight home was several hours away, and I had made a reservation at a motel near the airport. As Martin and I were parting, the loudspeaker announced that the motel bus was waiting for "Dr. Lomax." A Negro porter gathered my baggage and led me to the bus; he put my bags on the ground and I tipped him. A few seconds later I saw the white bus driver, and I knew I had reached a moment of confrontation. It seemed an eternity as I glanced up and down, from the white driver to my baggage; I remembered all those years I had spent serving white people as a bellboy, a shoeshine boy, a waiter. The driver, however, couldn't have cared less about me or my color. He picked up my bags and put them in the bus. This is what the Republic has done to me and twenty million like me—I never felt so equal in all my life when I saw that white man stoop down and pick up *my* bags. "Get right in, sir," he said.

The motel people were the same. They acted as if there had never been such a thing as segregation. I ate and drank where I pleased. Later I had to break away from three white men and their woman companion who latched onto me in the motel dining room and insisted that I party with them until my plane left.

II

I came back home to the land tilled and served by my fathers for four generations. Valdostans, like most people, are children of fixity;

as individuals and as a tribe they find a crag, a limb, a spot of earth—physical or emotional or both—and they cling on for dear life. They change without growing, and the more they change the more they remain the same. What frightens them, as with most people, is the sudden discovery that what they are—how they have lived all their lives—stands somehow in the path of history and of progress.

One can go home again if he remembers and accepts the land of his birth for what it was, if he understands what that land has become and why. The homecoming is more complete if one admits that he and his land have shaped each other, that from it springs much of both his weakness and his strength. Only as I walked down River Street toward the place I was born did I realize how much of a child of this land I am: its mud squished through my toes as I romped on unpaved streets and alleys; its puritanical somnolence settled over my childhood dreams and all but choked me into conformity. It was on the corner of River and Wells streets, when I was eight years old, that a white man ordered his bulldog to attack me simply because I was a Negro. Judge J. G. Cranford and his wife lived in the big white house on the corner. They saw the incident from the front porch, and Mrs. Cranford ran into the street to my rescue and drove the man away with shame.

River Street has grown old without changing very much. The weed field that stretched between here and Jackson Street Lane is still a weed field; the old warehouse that sat at the edge of the field is now a surplus food distribution center. The houses are the same houses they were when I was a child.

R. F. Lewes, as I shall call him, lived on this block. The summer before my junior year in college I was a handyman in his shop. Mr. Lewes would entertain his customers with dramatic descriptions of lynchings he had attended. His favorite story was about the night three Negroes were killed in a swamp near the Florida line. Lewes would advise his customers to get to a lynching early and stake out a choice spot on the killing ground. "But if the crowd is already there when you get there," he would add, "get down on your all fours and crawl between their legs so you can get up close to the nigger." One night I was cleaning the store when three of Mr. Lewes's cronies came in. "By God," he said to them, "this has been a rough day. Let's get a pint of moonshine and find some nigger bitches and get our luck changed."

Finally the stories became too much, and one day I threw down my shoeshine rag and went home. (After all, I was almost a junior in college and an official in my campus NAACP.) Lewes's son drove to our house and insisted that I return to work. My grandfather, the minister of the Macedonia First African Baptist Church, flatly said I didn't have to work in a place where my race was abused. R. F. Lewes, Jr., assured Grandfather that he would see to it that his father stopped telling lynch stories while I was in the shop. I had hardly returned to work when Lewes walked up to me and put his arms around my shoulders. "Louis," he said, eying me as if I were a wounded animal, "I wouldn't hurt *you!*"

During my visit home I saw Mr. Lewes on the street. He is very old and walks with a stick. A few weeks before, a Negro man had sat on a bench on the courthouse lawn next to him. Recoiling in anger, Lewes began jabbing the Negro in the ribs with his walking stick. The Negro called the police, and they told Lewes that the courthouse bench was for all the people, and either to calm down or move on. Mr. Lewes moved on.

III

Ours was a curious ghetto. Jackson Street Lane was the boundary line between the Negro and white sections along River Street. For one block Negroes lived on the north side of the street; the south side was completely white. To compound the oddness—the kind of thing that keeps the South on the thin edge of insanity—the first two families in our block were white. I remember how their menfolk ran into the street rejoicing the night Max Schmeling defeated Joe Louis.

The two white houses are still there, but I cannot for the life of me account for the white people who had lived in them. They were of another world; I did not know their names, who they were, or what they did. For that matter, I can't recall a single white person in the entire town whom I *really knew* when I was a boy. There were a few white people—R. F. Lewes and the man whose bulldog attacked me—whom I truly feared and, more than likely, hated. There were a few white people, Mrs. Cranford for example, whom I trusted and, perhaps, loved. But whatever understanding I had of all of these people was based on nothing more than surface encounter.

The house where I was born is torn down, the land covered with brush. The corner grocery store, built by a grocery chain on land leased from my grandfather, is now an eyesore and a public hazard. This land still belongs to us. My Uncle James, now the preacher at the Macedonia Baptist Church, and I are the last of the Lomaxes. Soon we must sit down and decide what to do about the land. Where my grandmother's living room once was, there are wild weeds; thistles cover the place where my grandfather used to retire on Saturday nights to prepare his sermon. There are tall bushes in the potato patch and creeping vines in the bait bed.

There are other changes. The new freeway that runs from Atlanta to Jacksonville has ruined the sucker and catfish hole where Grandfather and I used to fish. The new city hall and its grounds sprawl over the homesites of more than twenty families, Negro and white. The mud swamp on the Clydesville Road is now the airport, and the Dasher High School from which I graduated twenty-five years ago is now the J. L. Lomax Junior High School, which is named after my Uncle James.

When I walked these streets as a boy I prided myself in the fact that I knew exactly how many people there were in the town— 14,592. (My grandfather used to say that this figure included "Negroes, white people, chickens, cows, two mules, and a stray hound dog.") By 1960 the population had more than doubled, and it is predicted that there may be 75,000 people living here by 1980. Since I was a child the number of people working in agriculture has decreased threefold; the corresponding increase in trades, technical, professional, and government employees is expected to continue.

Despite the occasional new sight, Valdosta, like most American cities and towns, is old and tired and falling down. A few weeks before, not far from my old home, a chimney fell from a dilapidated building and killed a small child. In October of 1964 the city manager pleaded with the mayor and the city council for power to initiate a comprehensive housing code. His research showed that 33 per cent of Valdosta's housing is either dilapidated or deteriorating, that less than half of the town's dwelling units are owner-occupied, and that only slightly more than five hundred new housing units will be erected during the rest of the 1960s. The city manager wanted to force the owners of deteriorating properties to fix them up, the owners of dilapidated buildings to tear them down under the threat that if they don't the city will. He wanted to do something about the lack of recreational facilities for young people. So far he has not succeeded, but he is still trying.

A referendum that would have levied two bond issues for parks and recreation was defeated, with about 10 per cent of the registered voters participating. But some time later a one-million-dollar school bond issue won the voters' approval, although less than two thousand of the city's eight thousand registered women voters bothered to go to the polls.

Apathy plagues the town. The people, both Negro and white, seem to have run out of gas. They simply don't care about civic improvements. The referendum for parks and recreation would have given the city two swimming pools. It was defeated by seventeen votes. Yet one night I walked up and down Patterson Street, the white mecca, and saw scores of boys and girls slinking into darkened store alcoves and alleys. Then I went down along South Ashley Street, the Negro section, and saw even more young people darting into back streets, petting in open lots, dancing to funky music in questionable "soda and ice cream parlors."

IV

As far as public accommodations go, Valdosta is an open town. I ate where I chose and went where I pleased, talking with whomever I wished of both races. Like most Southern towns, this one had moments of racial tension during the first days of integrated cafés, lunch counters, and theaters. But a well-disciplined law force invoked the law of the land. While police chiefs in other Southern towns were rousing the white rabble, the Valdosta police chief was traveling through the swamp farmlands on the town's outskirts telling white men who were most likely to get likkered up and come to town to keep calm. The Negroes were told to eat, not just demonstrate, and the whites were warned to keep the peace. They both did just that. Whenever and wherever Negroes have pressed their case there has been compliance with the 1964 Civil Rights Act.

This did not happen all by itself. A loosely organized interracial council arrived at reasonable, step-by step goals. I think the major preventive act took place when the white power structure yielded to demands for Negro policemen. The sight of Negroes whom they knew and trusted policing their community gave Valdosta's Negroes a pride and a sense of personal security they had never had before. My town has not made ugly national and international headlines because the white power structure, led by three key men, took a long look at the turmoil that confronted so many places in the South and decided it would not happen in Valdosta.

E. M. Turner, the seventy-two-year-old editor of the local paper, took the same position with me. I was both astounded and angry. He had been the editor of the paper since I was a child. I had wanted to be a reporter and a writer, to learn the fundamentals of my craft, but I couldn't even get a job as a delivery boy. The first essay I ever wrote won me an honorable mention in a contest sponsored by the paper; they announced that I was a Negro and they misspelled my name. Yet E. M. Turner sat with me now for almost an hour and a half. He traced the rise of Valdosta from a one-crop town that trembled at the thought of the boll weevil to a town which changed its economy to one based on turpentine, pine trees, and resin. He sketched out the semi-industrial era that lies ahead for the town.

Our talk moved on to the race issue. "I've never had any trouble with nigras," Turner said. "I may not like the Civil Rights Bill, but it's the law of the land and it must be obeyed. But let me tell you this," he said. "I talked to my cook; she is a sweet old nigra woman who has been with us for years and she told me she didn't want her grandchildren going to school with white children."

I heard E. M. Turner well, and I thought to myself that I have yet to meet a white man, in the South or the North, whose cook believed in integration. Yet I wondered how, without integrated schools, such a man as Turner expected us to turn out Negroes equally prepared for the American job market. I decided to ask a significant question:

"Would you hire a Negro reporter if he was qualified?"

Turner did not hesitate. "I've never been faced with the issue," he said. "I'm not sure what I would do."

Later that day, when I had a talk with a local businessman, I saw something of the anguish that afflicts many white Valdostans of my age. His brother-in-law lives in Colombia and is married to a Colombian woman darker than most Negroes. The brother wanted to bring his wife to Valdosta for a visit; the proposed visit was, of course, vetoed with vigor. "Lord, how ashamed I am," he told me. "I'm afraid to have my own brother and sister come to my home."

He is a devout member of a Protestant Church in Valdosta. His church raises money each month to keep an impoverished Negro church of the same denomination going. "We raise that money," he told me, "to keep the Negroes from coming to our church. I was just horrified when I saw how my fellow white Christians reacted when the question of integrating the two churches came up."

But it was another realization that really troubled him. "Now take you," he said. "I'd like to have you in my home, to sit down to prayer and break bread with my family. My wife feels the same way. But we'd be afraid to invite you."

"I'd invite you to my home," I told him. "I'm not afraid."

"But I'd be afraid to *come*," he shot back, pounding the desk with anger at his world and himself.

"In other words," I said, "there is a sense in which I, a Negro, have more freedom than you have."

"That's true," he replied. "Everything is so confused down here. They wouldn't bother you and your Uncle James if you invited my family to your home. But they would get after *us* if we came." He turned in his chair, dropping me out of his sight as he faced the wall and let his eyes drift toward the ceiling.

"But I did vote for Goldwater," he added, speaking more to himself than to me. "Somebody has just got to stop the Communists from taking over the world."

V

The 1964 Goldwater victory hung like a frightening cloud over the well-meaning white Valdostans who were trying to find a way out of the racial wilderness. One of the men most responsible for Goldwater's carrying Valdosta was George C. Cook, the seventy-three-year-old owner of the radio station. Cook came to town thirty years ago and became a leader in the business community; he has been president of the Chamber of Commerce and has spearheaded the drive to get more industry—"particularly those that will give these nigger women on relief something to do," he explained to me—into Valdosta. He made his station the voice of Goldwater conservatism and the White Citizens' Council. The week before the election, Cook encountered one of Valdosta's most respected Negroes in the post office. "Doctor," Cook said to the Negro, "I want you to go home and call all your friends and tell them to tune in on my station tonight at seven-thirty. We're going to give the niggers and Jews hell tonight and I sure want you and your people to hear it."

I talked with Cook for more than an hour. "Now I came out for Goldwater, but I ain't no Republican," he said. "I'm a Democrat. That," he went on to say, pounding his chest, "is in here, in my heart. I could no more be a Republican than I could fly. But I just couldn't stomach that Kennedy-Johnson crowd and the way they are taking over the rights of the states and the individual.

"Now as for this integration business, I don't see what all the hell's about. We never had any trouble with niggers. I was against the Civil Rights Bill but when it became the law of the land I felt we'd better try and live with it. One of my friends called me up and told me he'd gotten word that the niggers were coming to his lunch counter to demonstrate. He said he was going to feed them if they came there. I told him, by God, to feed them niggers and he'd find out that once he fed them, and they had made their point, they would never come back. And you know," he added, bursting into laughter, "that's exactly what happened. Them niggers ate, then they left and ain't a one of them black sonsabitches been back there since.

"Let me tell you something, Louis," he said suddenly. "I lived with niggers all my life; I grew up with them and played with them; there wasn't a bit of trouble. Why a sweet, old black nigger woman helped raise me; she was as sweet a woman as God ever let live. And if and when I get to heaven I'm going to look up that nigger woman and kiss her on the cheek.

"There ain't going to be no trouble here," he said. "A few young niggers and young white trash might try to start something; then the old heads, nigger and white, will keep things under control. What we need in this town instead of agitation is some new industries with nigger jobs, so these nigger men can feed their families, so these nigger women on relief can make a pay check. That's what we need to keep Valdosta going. Why, the niggers are pouring into town by the carloads every day, and if we don't find something for them to do we are going to have one hell of a mess in this town before too long. Yes sir, that's what this town needs: nigger jobs, for nigger men and women."

On the subject of jobs, Comer Cherry, a diametrical opposite to Cook among the business community, feels the same way. Cherry has been president of the Chamber of Commerce and the Rotary Club, and a prime mover behind the biracial commission. He is representative of the new thinking among white Valdostans. "The way I see it," he says, "the economy of the nigra community is the root of the problem. Once the nigra can earn a respectable pay check, most of the agitation will die down."

The median income for a Valdosta white family in 1960 was

$4,360; for Valdosta Negro families, $2,364. And there is a chilling prophecy in a recent economic study of the town. The study predicts that by 1980 the median income of Valdosta white families will be $9,500, while the income of Negro families will reach only $4,250 —more than twice the present disparity. Comer Cherry and George C. Cook have a point. Somebody, somehow, had better do something about Negro income in Valdosta or there could be real trouble in the future.

VI

I found no tension whatsoever in the Valdosta Negro community. The Negro masses undulate along the streets, oblivious to what is going on in the Congo, in Red China, or in Mississippi. The county hospital has been completely integrated, and the authorities have shut down the old back entrance marked "colored." Yet despite the fact that the leaders have told local Negroes to use the front door, one witnesses the pathetic spectacle of their going to the same place to find a back way in. What mainly struck me is that there are more of them, and that they are growing in geometric proportions. They are the citizens of "Niggertown," the habitués of juke joints, of pig-foot alley and crumbling shanties. Their children pour into school, only to drop out. Talking with these dropouts one comes away knowing that they never really dropped in. They don't know anything; they can't do anything. Here, among the black masses, is the greatest monument to my town's—the South's—wickedness. It is a society which continues to grind out hundreds, thousands, millions who are totally defeated, who are alienated from that society from the day they are born.

The Valdosta black bourgeoisie serve the black masses. They teach them in school, pull their teeth, prescribe medicine for their livers, tell them about Jesus on Sunday morning, sell them life insurance when they are young, and bury them when they die. That is the way it was thirty-five years ago; that is the way it is now. Their only saving grace—and this is true all over the country—is that they are willing to accept, without recourse to background, any person who can traverse the maze that leads from Shantytown to professionalism. I was born to the black bourgeoisie; I stumbled and floundered for twenty years; and there were grave doubts that I would ever validate my heritage. Yet I had schoolmates who were up from the trash pile; some of them made it, and they are now solid members of the Valdosta Negro middle class.

It would be wrong for me to say that they don't care about the black masses. They do care; they care, at times, almost to the point of nervous breakdown. Their problem, essentially, is the same as that of the concerned white men of Valdosta: the monster created by the Southern way of life is so terrifying, and becoming so gargantuan, that nobody knows what to do or where to start doing it.

Meanwhile, the Valdosta black bourgeoisie are becoming more and more comfortable, their world more and more secure. They are the ones who can afford to dress up and go out for dinner once a week to a previously "white only" restaurant, who can travel during their vacations and take advantage of the integrated motels, hotels, and travel facilities. Yet few of them have actually contributed to the Negro revolution that has made these things possible. The Valdosta black bourgeoisie are largely schoolteachers. Despite their new freedom, they must plod away in school rooms that are still separate and unequal; they must keep quiet about integration or be fired.

"I'm doing all I can do and still keep my job," one third-grade Negro teacher told me. "When my principal isn't around, I teach my children that four pickets times nine pickets is thirty-six pickets. I just hope and pray they grow up and get the message."

Part of the tragedy of my town is that there is no real Negro leadership to translate to the masses the message this teacher is trying to deliver. Negro leadership in Valdosta is nothing more than ten or twelve men with incomes rooted in the ghetto, who sporadically gather to try to muster general support for programs each of them has presented to the town's white fathers when his fellow Negro spokesmen were not looking. A dozen of these Negro leaders—most of whom I have known since childhood—met with me to discuss the plight of the Valdosta Negro and to describe what they planned to do about it. The more they talked the more it became apparent, as one of them had the courage to say, that Negro leadership was about the same as it was when I was a little boy. There is no NAACP in Valdosta, no Urban League. Nobody would dare let Martin Luther King, Jr., preach in their church, and CORE is something they read about in the newspaper and hear about on television. The Negro leaders, such as they are, turn on each other and accuse one another of being disloyal, apathetic, and indifferent.

VII

What, then, is the next step forward for Valdosta, not just toward integration, but into the world as it really is?

Although the Negro population is 36 per cent, as of the summer of 1965 not a single public school was integrated in the town. However, the all-white board of education is ready to accept Negro pupils into any schools they can establish their legal right to attend. Moreover, the white power structure knows precisely where these schools are, and the white students have been prepared for the probability that their schools will one day be integrated. Even more, the white students have accepted the idea and wish the Negroes would get it over with so everybody concerned can settle down to learning his lessons.

White Valdosta businessmen have jobs waiting for Negroes; these jobs will never be filled until Negro leaders stop fighting each other and draw up a unified job program to place before the biracial commission.

At a state college located in Valdosta, I was told, there were only two Negro students, and these were financed by some of the Negro leaders who met with me. No other Negroes had enrolled in two years. This could be changed if Negro spokesmen would unify and make the right demands. There is an integrated county technical and industrial school on the outskirts of Valdosta that is begging for Negro students. There are all too few Negro applicants. The brunt of the burden, I regret to say, rests with the town's Negro middle class. But they, like so many of their white peers, are consumed by fear.

The Valdosta Negro middle class, then, is on the verge of becoming a tribe; its members are fiercely proud of themselves and their own; they couldn't care less about socializing with white people. At a large party given for me one night, I was able to locate only one Negro friend—a woman—who had a social relationship with a white person. She and a white woman have a "luncheon friendship," largely at the urging of the white woman. Even that almost collapsed when the white woman invited other white women to join.

"The other white women smiled dryly at me," she said, "and I was ready to say, like, forget it. My husband makes more than her husband and I wasn't about to grovel just to have some white lunch dates."

"I know what you mean," a county school principal said. "These phony white liberals are about a bitch. They say they love us, that they want to cement relations, that they want to overcome the fact that there has been no communication between us and them, and then they get in that damn voting booth and. . . ."

"Vote for Goldwater," several people shouted.

"You think you got problems," a doctor broke in. "I was walking down Patterson Street a few weeks ago and a white man fell to the sidewalk with a heart attack right in front of me. I forgot he was white and tried to help him. A crowd gathered and became hostile because I was a Negro!"

"Did you go away and let him die?" somebody shouted from the back of the room.

"No," the doctor replied, "I did the best I could for the sonofabitch and sent him off to the hospital." Everyone, of course, laughed.

The party music played, but there was surprisingly little drinking or dancing. I was home; these were my brothers and sisters. They knew me and were glad to see me. We talked of the days when we were children, of our fathers and mothers and grandparents who pushed us so far along the way. We told the "in" jokes. Nobody mentioned white people; nobody wanted or needed them there. We would have stayed all night if it had not been Saturday. But at church the next morning one of the school principals was scheduled to sing a solo. One woman was to play the organ, another the piano. Another school principal was to handle the collection, and I was to deliver the sermon.

VIII

The next day I stood in the Macedonia Baptist Church pulpit that has been occupied by a Lomax for more than half a century; some of the people who sat in the congregation had known me before I knew myself. Tribal middle-class pride was running high. Just the Sunday before, Calvin King, one of my younger childhood schoolmates who went on to get his doctorate in mathematics, had been the guest preacher. Uncle James had listened with pride as Calvin told of his travels in the Holy Land, of his work in helping launch a new university in Nigeria.

I told the congregation about my experiences in Africa, behind the Iron Curtain, and in American cities where racial troubles had erupted. White Christianity, I said, had become synonymous with white oppression all over the world, and the black Christians were about all Jesus had left. We were the only ones who could now go about preaching the words of Jesus without being suspected of questionable motives. My plea was that we black Christians become more militant, that we take a courageous stand for human rights, to clarify Christ's name if for no other reason.

It is significant that when I had finished there was a loud congregational "amen." A few white people had come to the service, and one of them was crying. Uncle James issued the invitation for the unchurched to come up and join. But that was not the hour for sinners. Rather, I think, it was a time for the believers to reassess what they were in for.

Change is coming. Having seen many of the troubled places of Africa, America, and the Caribbean, I know social dynamite when I see it. But Valdosta will make it peacefully into tomorrow, partly because the whites themselves are slowly changing, partly because the Negroes are not really pushing. Time nudges them both along. They—the black and the white of my town—are now looking across at each other in estrangement against the day when they might join in frank friendship.

V

Mississippi: The Fallen Paradise

♦

by WALKER PERCY

A little more than one hundred years ago, a Mississippi regiment dressed its ranks and started across a meadow toward Cemetery Ridge, a minor elevation near Gettysburg. There, crouched behind a stone wall, the soldiers of the Army of the Potomac waited and watched with astonishment as the gray-clads advanced as casually as if they were on parade. The Mississippians did not reach the wall. One soldier managed to plant the regimental colors within an arm's length before he fell. The University Grays, a company made up of students from the state university, suffered a loss of precisely one hundred per cent of its members killed or wounded in the charge.

These were good men. It was an honorable fight and there were honorable men on both sides of it. The issue was settled once and for all, perhaps by this very charge. The honorable men on the losing side, men like General Lee, accepted the verdict.

One hundred years later, Mississippians were making history of a different sort. If their record in Lee's army is unsurpassed for valor and devotion to duty, present-day Mississippi is mainly renowned for murder, church-burning, dynamiting, assassination, night-riding, not to mention the lesser forms of terrorism. The students of the university celebrated the Centennial by a different sort of warfare and in the company of a different sort of General. It is not frivolous to compare the characters of General Edwin Walker and General Lee, for the contrast is symptomatic of a broader change in leadership in this part of the South. In any event, the major claim to fame of the present-day university is the Ole Miss football team and the assault of the student body upon the person of one man, an assault of bullying, spitting, and obscenities. The bravest Mississippians in recent years have not been Confederates or the sons of Confederates but rather two Negroes, James Meredith and Medgar Evers.

As for the Confederate flag, once the battle ensign of brave men, it has come to stand for raw racism and hoodlum defiance of the law. An art professor at Ole Miss was bitterly attacked for "desecrating" the Stars and Bars when he depicted the flag as it was used in the 1962 riot—with curses and obscenities. The truth was that it had been desecrated long before.

No ex-Mississippian is entitled to write of the tragedy which has overtaken his former state with any sense of moral superiority. For he cannot be certain in the first place that if he had stayed he would not have kept silent—or worse. And he strongly suspects that he would not have been counted among the handful, an editor here, a professor there, a clergyman yonder, who not only did not keep silent but fought hard.

What happened to this state? Assuredly it faced difficult times after the Supreme Court decision of 1954 and subsequent court injunctions which required painful changes in customs of long standing. Yet the change has been made peacefully in other states of the South. In Georgia before the 1965 voting bill was passed by Congress, over 39 per cent of Negroes of voting age were registered to vote. In Mississippi the figure was around 6 per cent.

What happened is both obvious and obscure. What is obvious is that Mississippi is poor, largely rural, and has in proportion the largest Negro minority in the United States. But Georgia shares these traits. Nor is it enough to say that Mississippi is the state that refused to change, although this is what one hears both inside and outside the state. On the contrary, Mississippi has changed several times since the Civil War. There have been times, for example, when dissent was not only possible but welcome. In 1882 George Washington Cable, novelist and ex-Confederate cavalryman, addressed the graduating class at the University of Mississippi:

We became distended—mired and stuffed with conservatism to the point of absolute rigidity. Our life had little or nothing to do with the onward movement of the world's thought. We were in danger of becoming a civilization that was not a civilization, because there was not in it the element of advancement.

His address was warmly received by the newspapers of the region. It is interesting to speculate how these remarks would be received today at Ole Miss, if indeed Cable would be allowed to speak at all.

Two significant changes have occurred in the past generation. The most spectacular is the total defeat of the old-style white moderate and the consequent collapse of the alliance between the "good" white man and the Negro, which has figured more or less prominently in Mississippi politics since Reconstruction days. Except for an oasis or two like Greenville, the influential white moderate is gone. To use Faulkner's *personae*, the Gavin Stevenses have disappeared and the Snopeses have won. What is more, the Snopeses' victory has surpassed even the gloomiest expectations of their creator. What happened to men like Gavin Stevens? With a few exceptions, they have shut up or been exiled or they are running the local White Citizens' Council. Not even Faulkner foresaw the ironic denouement of the tragedy: that the Compsons and Sartorises should not only be defeated by the Snopeses but that in the end they should join them.

Faulkner lived to see the defeat of his Gavin Stevens—the old-style good man, the humanist from Harvard and Heidelberg—but he still did not despair because he had placed his best hope in the youth of the state. Chick Mallison in *Intruder in the Dust*, a sort of latter-day Huck Finn, actually got the Negro Lucas Beauchamp out of jail while Gavin Stevens was talking about the old alliance. But this hope has been blasted, too. The melancholy fact is the Chick Mallisons today are apt to be the worst lot of all. Ten years of indoctrination by the Citizens' Councils, racist politicians, and the most one-sided press north of Cuba has produced a generation of good-looking and ferocious young bigots.

The other change has been the emigration of the Negro from Mississippi, reducing the Negro majority to a minority for the first time in a hundred years. At the same time great numbers of Negroes from the entire South were settling in Northern ghettos. The chief consequence has been the failure of the great cities of the North to deal with the Negro when he landed on their doorstep, or rather next door. Mississippi has not got any better, but New York and Boston and Los Angeles have got worse.

Meanwhile there occurred the Negro revolution, and the battle lines changed. For the first time in a hundred and fifty years, the old sectional division has been blurred. It is no longer "North" versus "South" in the argument over the Negro. Instead there has occurred a diffusion of the Negro and a dilution of the problem, with large sections of the South at least tolerating a degree of social change at the very time Northern cities were beginning to grumble seriously. It seems fair to describe the present national mood as a grudging inclination to redress the Negro's grievances—with the exception of a few areas of outright defiance like north Louisiana, parts of Alabama, and the state of Mississippi.

Words Without Meaning

It is only within the context of these social changes, I believe, that the state can be understood and perhaps some light shed upon a possible way out. For, unfavorable as these events may be, they are nevertheless ambiguous in their implication. The passing of the moderate and the victory of the Snopeses may be bad things in themselves. Yet history being the queer business that it is, such a turn of events may be the very condition of the state's emergence from its long nightmare.

During the past ten years Mississippi as a society reached a condition which can only be described, in an analogous but exact sense of the word, as insane. The rift in its character between a genuine kindliness and a highly developed individual moral consciousness on the one hand, and on the other a purely political and amoral view of "states' rights" at the expense of human rights led at last to a sundering of its very soul. Kind fathers and loving husbands, when they did not themselves commit crimes against the helpless, looked upon such crimes with indifference. Political campaigns, once the noblest public activity in the South, came to be conducted by incantation. The candidate who hollers nigger loudest and longest usually wins.

The language itself has been corrupted. In the Mississippi standard version of what happened, noble old English words are used, words like *freedom, sacredness of the individual, death to tyranny,* but they have subtly changed their referents. After the Oxford riot in 1962, the Junior Chamber of Commerce published a brochure entitled *A Warning for Americans,* which was widely distributed and is still to be found on restaurant counters in Jackson along with the usual racist tracts, mammy dolls, and Confederate flags. The pamphlet purports to prove that James Meredith was railroaded into Ole Miss by the Kennedys in defiance of "normal judicial processes"—a remarkable thesis in itself considering that the Meredith case received one of the most exhaustive judicial reviews in recent history. The "warning" for Americans was the usual contention that states' rights were being trampled by federal tyranny. "Tyranny is tyranny," reads the pamphlet. "It is the duty of every American to be alert when his freedom is endangered."

Lest the reader be complacent about Mississippi as the only state of double-think, the pamphlet was judged by the *national* Jay Cees to be the "second most worthy project of the year."

All statements become equally true and equally false, depending on one's rhetorical posture. In the end even the rhetoric fails to arouse. When Senator Eastland declares, "There is no discrimination in Mississippi," and, "All who are qualified to vote, black or white, exercise the right of suffrage," these utterances are received by friend and foe alike with a certain torpor of spirit. It does not matter that there is very little connection between Senator Eastland's utterances and the voting statistics of his home county: that of a population of 31,020 Negroes, 161 are registered to vote. Once the final break is made between language and reality, arguments generate their own force and lay out their own logical rules. The current syllogism goes something like this: (1) There is no ill-feeling in Mississippi between

the races; the Negroes like things the way they are; if you don't
believe it, I'll call my cook out of the kitchen and you can ask her.
(2) The trouble is caused by outside agitators who are communist-
inspired. (3) Therefore, the real issue is between atheistic commu-
nism and patriotic God-fearing Mississippians.

Once such a system cuts the outside wires and begins to rely on its
own feedback, anything becomes possible. The dimensions of the
tragedy are hard to exaggerate. The sad and still incredible fact is
that many otherwise decent people, perhaps even the majority of the
white people in Mississippi, honestly believed that President John F.
Kennedy was an enemy of the United States, if not a communist
fellow-traveler.

How did it happen that a proud and decent people, a Protestant
and Anglo-Saxon people with a noble tradition of freedom behind
them, should have in the end become so deluded that it is difficult
even to discuss the issues with them because the common words of
the language no longer carry the same meanings? How can responsible leadership have failed so completely when it did not fail in
Georgia, a state with a similar social and ethnic structure?

The answer is far from clear, but several reasons suggest themselves. For one thing, as James Dabbs points out in his recent book
Who Speaks for the South?, Mississippi was part of the wild west of
the Old South. Unlike the seaboard states, it missed the liberal eighteenth century altogether. Its tradition is closer to Dodge City than to
Williamsburg. For another, the Populism of the eastern South never
amounted to much here; it was corrupted from the beginning by the
demagogic racism of Vardaman and Bilbo. Nor did Mississippi have
its big city which might have shared, for good and ill, in the currents
of American urban life. Georgia had its Atlanta and Atlanta had the
good luck or good sense to put men like Ralph McGill and Mayor
Hartsfield in key positions. What was lacking in Mississippi was the
new source of responsible leadership, the political realists of the
matured city. The old moderate tradition of the planter-lawyer-
statesman class had long since lost its influence. The young industrial
interests have been remarkable chiefly for their discretion. When, for
example, they did awake to the folly of former Governor Barnett's

two-bit rebellion, it was too late. And so there was no one to head off the collision between the civil-rights movement and the racist coalition between redneck, demagogue, and small-town merchant. The result was insurrection.

Death of an Alliance

The major source of racial moderation in Mississippi even until recent times has been, not Populism, but the white conservative tradition with its peculiar strengths and, as it turned out, its fatal weakness. There came into being after Reconstruction an extraordinary alliance, which persisted more or less fitfully until the last world war, between the Negro and the white conservative, an alliance originally directed against the poor whites and the Radical Republicans. The fruits of this "fusion principle," as it is called, are surprising. Contrary to the current mythology of the Citizens' Councils, which depicts white Mississippians throwing out the carpetbaggers and Negroes and establishing our present "way of life" at the end of Reconstruction, the fact is that Negroes enjoyed considerably more freedom in the 1880s than they do now. A traveler in Mississippi after Reconstruction reported seeing whites and Negroes served in the same restaurants and at the same bars in Jackson.

This is not to say that there ever existed a golden age of race relations. But there were bright spots. It is true that the toleration of the Old Captains, as W. J. Cash called them, was both politically motivated and paternalistic, but it is not necessarily a derogation to say so. A man is a creature of his time—after all, Lincoln was a segregationist—and the old way produced some extraordinary men. There were many felicities in their relation with the Negro—it was not all Uncle Tomism, though it is unfashionable to say so. In any case they lost; segregation was firmly established around 1890 and lynch law became widespread. For the next fifty years the state was dominated, with a few notable exceptions, by a corrupt Populism.

What is important to notice here is the nature of the traditional alliance between the white moderate and the Negro, and especially the ideological basis of the former's moderation, because this spirit has informed the ideal of race relations for at least a hundred years. For, whatever its virtues, the old alliance did not begin to have the resources to cope with the revolutionary currents of this century. Indeed the world view of the old-style "good" man is almost wholly irrelevant to the present gut issue between the Negro revolt and the Snopes counterrevolution.

For one thing, the old creed was never really social or political but purely and simply moral in the Stoic sense: if you are a good man, then you will be magnanimous toward other men and especially toward the helpless and therefore especially toward the Negro. The Stoic creed worked very well—if you were magnanimous. But if one planter was just, the next might charge 80 per cent interest at the plantation store, the next take the wife of his tenant, the next lease convict labor, which was better than the sharecropper system because it did not matter how hard you worked your help or how many died.

Once again in recent years dissent became possible. During the depression of the 1930s and afterward there were stirrings of liberal currents not only in the enthusiasm for the economic legislation of the Roosevelt Administration but also in a new awareness of the plight of the Negro. Mississippi desperately needed the New Deal and profited enormously from it. Indeed, the Roosevelt farm program succeeded too well. Planters who were going broke on ten cent cotton voted for Roosevelt, took federal money, got rich, lived to hate Kennedy and Johnson and vote for Goldwater—while still taking federal money. Yet there was something new in the wind after the war. Under the leadership of men like Hodding Carter in the Delta, a new form of racial moderation began to gather strength. Frank Smith, author of the book *Congressman from Mississippi*, was elected to Congress. Described by Edward Morgan as "a breath of fresh air out of a political swamp," Smith was one of the few politicians in recent years who tried to change the old racial refrain and face up to the real problems of the state. But he made the mistake of voting for such radical measures as the Peace Corps and the United Nations appropriation, and he did not conceal his friendship with President Kennedy. What was worse, he addressed mail to his constituents with a Mr. and Mrs., even when they were Negroes. Smith was euchred out of his district by the legislature and defeated in 1962 by the usual coalition of peckerwoods, super-patriots, and the Citizens' Councils.

But the most radical change has occurred in the past few years. As recently as fifteen years ago, the confrontation was still a three-cornered one, among the good white man, the bad white man, and the Negro. The issue was whether to treat the Negro well or badly. It went without saying that you could do either. Now one of the parties has been eliminated and the confrontation is face to face. "I assert my right to vote and to raise my family decently," the Negro is beginning to say. His enemies reply with equal simplicity: "We'll kill you first."

Yet the victory of the Snopeses is not altogether a bad thing. At least the choice is clarified. It would not help much now to have Gavin Stevens around with his talk about "man's struggle to the stars."

The old way is still seductive, however, and evokes responses from strange quarters. Ex-Governor Ross Barnett was recently revealed as mellow emeritus statesman in the old style, even hearkening to the antique summons of noblesse oblige. A newspaper interview reported that the Governor was a soft touch for any Negro who waylaid him in the corridor with a "Cap'n, I could sho use a dollar." The Governor, it was also reported, liked to go hunting with a Negro friend. "We laugh and joke," the Governor reminisced, "and he gets a big kick out of it when I call him Professor. There's a lot in our relationship I can't explain." No doubt, mused the interviewer, the Governor would get up at all hours of the night to get Ol' Jim out of jail. It is hard to imagine what Gavin Stevens would make of this new version of the old alliance. Unquestionably something new has been added. When Marse Ross dons the mantle of Marse Robert, Southern history has entered upon a new age. And perhaps it is just as well. Let Governor Barnett become the new squire. It simplifies matters further.

Public vs. Private

Though Faulkner liked to use such words as "cursed" and "doomed" in speaking of his region, it is questionable that Mississippians are very different from other Americans. It is increasingly less certain that Minnesotans would have performed better under the circumstances. There is, however, one peculiar social dimension wherein the state does truly differ. It has to do with the distribution, as Mississippians see it, of what is public and what is private. More precisely it is the absence of a truly public zone, as the word is understood in most places. One has to live in Mississippi to appreciate it. No doubt it is the mark of an almost homogeneous white population, a Protestant Anglo-Saxon minority (until recently), sharing a common tragic past and bound together by kinship bonds. This society was not only felicitous in many ways; it also commanded the allegiance of Southern intellectuals on other grounds. Faulkner saw it as the chief bulwark against the "coastal spew of Europe" and "the rootless ephemeral cities of the North." In any case, the almost familial ambit of this society came to coincide with the actual public space which it inhabited. The Negro was either excluded, shoved off into Happy Hollow, or admitted to the society on its own terms as good old Uncle Ned. No allowance was made—it would have been surprising if there had been— for a truly public sector, unlovely as you please and defused of emotional charges, where black and white might pass without troubling each other. The whole of the Delta, indeed of white Mississippi, is one big kinship lodge. You have only to walk into a restaurant or a bus station to catch a whiff of it. There is a sudden kindling of amiability, even between strangers. The salutations, "What you say now?" and "Yall be good," are exchanged like fraternal signs. The presence of fraternity and sorority houses at Ole Miss always seemed oddly superfluous.

One consequence of this peculiar social structure has been a chronic misunderstanding between the state and the rest of the country. The state feels that unspeakable demands are being made upon it while the nation is bewildered by the response of rage to what seem to be the ordinary and minimal requirements of the law. Recall, for example, President Kennedy's gentle appeal to the university the night of the riot when he invoked the tradition of L. Q. C. Lamar and asked the students to do their duty even as he was doing his. He had got his facts straight about the tradition of valor in Mississippi. But unfortunately, the Kennedys had no notion of the social and semantic rules they were up against. When they entered into negotiations with the Governor to get Meredith on the campus, they proceeded on the reasonable assumption that even in the arena of political give and take—*i.e.*, deals—words bear some relation to their referents. Such was not the case. Governor Barnett did not doublecross the Kennedys in the usual sense. The double cross, like untruth, bears a certain relation to the truth. More serious, however, was the cultural confusion over the word "public." Ole Miss is not, or was not, a public school as the word is usually understood. In Mississippi as in England a public school means a private school. When Meredith finally did walk the paths at Ole Miss, his fellow students cursed and reviled him. But they also wept with genuine grief. If was as if he had been quartered in their living room.

It is this hypertrophy of pleasant familial space at the expense of a truly public sector which accounts for the extraordinary apposition in Mississippi of kindliness and unspeakable violence. Recently a tourist wrote the editor of the Philadelphia, Mississippi, newspaper that, although he expected the worst when he passed through the town, he found the folks in Philadelphia as nice as they could be. No doubt it is true. The Philadelphia the tourist saw is as pleasant as he said. It is like one big front porch.

A Place to Start

How can peace be restored to Mississippi? One would like to be able to say that the hope lies in putting into practice the Judeo-Christian ethic. In the end, no doubt, it does. But the trouble is that Christendom of a sort has already won in Mississippi. There is more church news in the Jackson papers than news about the Ole Miss football team. Political cartoons defend God against the Supreme Court. On the outskirts of Meridian a road sign announces: "The

Largest Percentage of Churchgoers in the World." It is a religion, however, which tends to canonize the existing social and political structure and to brand as atheistic any threat of change. "The trouble is they took God out of everything," said W. Arsene Dick of Summit, Mississippi, founder of Americans for the Preservation of the White Race. A notable exception to the general irrelevance of religion to social issues is the recent action of Millsaps College, a Methodist institution in Jackson, which voluntarily opened its doors to Negroes.

It seems more likely that progress will come about—as indeed it is already coming about—not through the impact of the churches upon churchgoers but because after a while the ordinary citizen gets sick and tired of the climate of violence and of the odor of disgrace which hangs over his region. Money has a good deal to do with it too; money, urbanization, and the growing concern of politicians and the business community with such things as public images. Governor Johnson occasionally talks sense. Last year the Mayor and the business leaders of Jackson defied the Citizens' Councils and supported the token desegregation of the schools. It could even happen that Governor Johnson, the man who campaigned up and down the state with the joke about what NAACP means (niggers, alligators, apes, coons, possums), may turn out to be the first Governor to enforce the law. For law enforcement, it is becoming increasingly obvious, is the condition of peace. It is also becoming more likely every day that federal intervention, perhaps in the form of local commissioners, may be required in places like Neshoba County where the Ku Klux Klan has been in control and law enforcement is a shambles. Faulkner at last changed his mind about the durability of the old alliance and came to prefer even enforced change to a state run by the Citizens' Councils and the Klan. Mississippians, he wrote, will not accept change until they have to. Then perhaps they will at last come to themselves: "Why didn't someone tell us this before? Tell us this in time?"

Much will depend on the residue of good will in the state. There are some slight signs of the long overdue revolt of the ordinary prudent man. There must be a good many of this silent breed. Hazel

Brannon Smith, who won a Pulitzer Prize as editor of the Lexington *Advertiser*, recently reported that in spite of all the abuse and the boycotts, the circulation of the paper continues to rise. The Mississippi Economic Council, the state's leading businessmen's group, issued a statement urging compliance with the 1964 Civil Rights Act and demanding that registration and voting laws be "fairly and impartially administered for all." In McComb several hundred leading citizens, after a reign of terror which lasted for a good part of 1964, demanded not only law and order but "equal treatment under the law for all citizens."

It may be that the corner has been turned. Mississippi, in the spring of 1965, looks better than Alabama. But who can say what would have happened if Martin Luther King had chosen Greenwood instead of Selma? Mississippi may in fact *be* better just because of Selma—though at this very writing Ole Miss students are living up to form and throwing rocks at Negroes. Nor can one easily forget the 1964 national election. The bizarre seven-to-one margin in favor of Senator Goldwater attests to the undiminished obsession with race. It would not have mattered if Senator Goldwater had advocated the collectivization of the plantations and open saloons in Jackson; he voted against the 1964 Civil Rights Bill and that was that.

Yet there is little doubt that Mississippi is even now beginning to feel its way toward what might be called the American Settlement of the racial issue, a somewhat ambiguous state of affairs which is less a solution than a more or less tolerable impasse. There has come into being an entire literature devoted to an assault upon the urban life wherein this settlement is arrived at, and a complete glossary of terms, such as alienation, depersonalization, and mass man. But in the light of recent history in Mississippi, the depersonalized American neighborhood looks more and more tolerable. A giant supermarket or eighty thousand people watching a pro ball game may not be the most creative of institutions, but at least they offer a *modus vivendi*. People generally leave each other alone.

A Southerner may still hope that some day the Southern temper, black and white, might yet prove to be the sociable yeast to leaven the American lump. Indeed he may suspect in his heart of hearts that the solution, if it comes, may have to come from him and from the South. And with good reason: the South, with all the monstrous mythologizing of its virtues, nevertheless has these virtues—a manner and a grace and a gift for human intercourse. And despite the humbuggery about the perfect love and understanding between us white folks and darkies down in Dixie, whites and blacks in the South do in fact know something about getting along with each other which the rest of the country does not know. Both black and white Southerner can help the country a great deal, though neither may choose to do so; the Negro for fear of being taken for Uncle Tom, the white from simple vengefulness: all right, Yankee, you've been preaching at us for a hundred years and now you've got them and you're making a mess of it and it serves you right. It may well come to lie with the South in the near future, as it lay with the North in 1860, to save the Union in its own way. Given enough trouble in New York and Chicago, another ten years of life in the subways and urine in the streets, it might at last dawn on him, the Southerner, that it is not the South which is being put upon but the *country* which is in trouble. Then he will act as he acted in 1916 and 1941.

Some day a white Mississippian is going to go to New York, make the usual detour through Harlem, and see it for the foul cheerless warren that it is; and instead of making him happy as it does now, it is going to make him unhappy. Then the long paranoia, this damnable sectional insanity, will be one important step closer to being over.

VI

A Conservative Prophecy:
Peace Below, Tumult Above
♦

by James Jackson Kilpatrick

Appomattox sleeps eighty miles to the west of Richmond. The unpretentious house where Lee surrendered, now a national shrine, sits on a small knoll, the grass clipped, the fences all in neat repair. Few visitors come; the parking lot is seldom filled. Beyond the park area lies the rolling country of Southside Virginia. In the autumn the leaves form a Persian carpet, dull reds, dark greens, lemon yellows, stretching as far as the eye can see. In the spring the view from the porch is of dogwoods soft as whitecaps in a pale green sea. There is indeed, as Bruce Catton wrote, a stillness here. The windows of McLean House gaze blankly on the countryside Lee saw a century ago; an old cannon, frozen like a setter on point, is no more than harmless heraldry. Here the fighting stopped.

Some months ago, in the fall, I drove past Appomattox, and paused to look around before driving on. Two days later, business took me to New York and, on impulse, I went through the teeming streets of Harlem. The bleak afternoon was heavy with the threat of rain, and the dark faces on the sidewalks seemed charged with the same oppressiveness. "This is where the riot was," the cab driver said. He was being informative, a good host. Here in Harlem, I reflected, the fighting goes on.

The stillness of Appomattox, and the noise of rioting in Harlem, speak of a contrast too sharp to go unmarked. My thesis is the improving health of the South and the sickness of the North, the rising hope for peace below the Potomac, the certain prospect of tumult above. The time approaches—it will come as surely as the tides—when the South will solve its racial problems and contrive, for white and black alike, a not intolerable way of life. And this hour will come while the bottles still rain from the tenement roofs of Harlem.

Three premises support my argument. One arises out of history, another from economics, a third from contemporary politics. Together they speak of a better South evolving.

What does the South bring to the racial crisis of our time? The overlooked answer is that it first brings these hundred years since Appomattox; and it brings more than two hundred years before that. Alone among the regions of this country, the South has lived with the Negro—lived in terms of massive "integration," in town and country and city, in love and hate, hostility and affection, indifference and concern. And the Negro has also lived with the South, grown used to its many faces, fashioned patterns of existence. All our lives we have known the same landmarks. Plowing through our storms we look up now and then and catch a glimpse of something shared. We have mapped old points to steer by. And if the Negro's legacy has also been that of indignity and hurt, we all of us have a mixed inheritance of good and ill. The white Southerner's life is no bed of gardenias either.

In many ways, these years have been fearfully hard on the Southern Negro. The Southern white man is just beginning to comprehend his own cruelties. The grim record of humiliation, insult, deprivation, and injustice, never having been sufficiently understood by the white South, is only now being acknowledged in this same quarter. But if the years have been hard in many ways, they have not been hard in all, and I suspect this truth is not generally perceived beyond the Potomac. Happiness for the Southern Negro is not necessarily a desegregated unit in a public housing project in New York. Disgraceful as the awful thought may seem, happiness can be a soft afternoon on the banks of the bayou, with the sun warm and the catfish biting.

I know, I know: it will be said that the pervading sin of the South's treatment of the Negro, tainting every hour, is the denial of self-respect, the inescapable stain of discrimination based upon color. "The Negro does not want the public housing unit," we are told. "He wants only to be treated as a human being." Precisely so. But in large areas of his everyday life, the Southern Negro has for years lived, loved, worked, and played as a human being, and if he has known much hurt and misery, he has known much happiness too. Along the banks of the bayou, all fishermen are equal. There may be discrimination in the morning and discrimination in the evening, but life also knows its long and placid afternoons. Today's doctrinaire abolitionists do not understand this. They have not caught enough catfish.

What have these more than three hundred years of living together taught the Southern white man of his black brother? James Baldwin's reply is "nothing at all." I believe, on the contrary, that the white man has learned a good deal; he is learning more, in new and more significant ways, and the pace of his learning is accelerating. At the very least, these generations of living together have dulled the edge of novelty. Many areas of the United States are just now experiencing a sudden consciousness of race. The phenomenal Negro migration from South to North is chiefly a development of the past twenty years. Call it prejudice, or call it human nature, or call it what you will, the interracial adjustment of white persons to Negro persons, in large numbers, takes time—more time than twenty years. The South has experienced this time, and doubtless in some ways the South has used it poorly. But Rochester never had known the time. By and large, its Negro people had no sense of roots, no sense of place. They did not share in that love of one's community which is the first link, as Burke said, in the series by which we proceed toward a love to our country, and to mankind.

Small Expectations

The South—and here I mean the whole of the white and Negro South—has learned this too: we have learned not to expect too much of one another. This is a lesson, elementary in human relationships, which the rest of the country has yet to master fully. Doubtless it is an oversimplification to say that the white employer expects his Negro hand to be shiftless, and is pleasantly amazed at evidence of industry; while the Negro worker expects his white boss to treat him as an inferior, and is pleasantly astonished to sense no sign of racial prejudice. I do not intend to be unkind; I do intend to be realistic, and the realities are that, in a great many economic activities, Negro workers as a group simply are not as reliable or as intelligent as white workers as a group. The building contractor who uses Negro labor, as Southern builders do, automatically contracts on a Monday morning for 10 or 20 per cent above the normal working force, because experience has taught him that 10 or 20 per cent of his colored hands will not show up. He condones this mild delinquency, because he understands that nothing whatever is to be gained by firing the missing men. They will be back of a Tuesday. And life goes on.

The years have taught the white South other lessons. It is fashionable these days to insist that racial characteristics as such do not exist. Out of its history, the South would deny this. We have learned, or think we have learned, something of the Negro's great capacity for patience, loyalty, humor, and affection. And perhaps we have learned, with exasperation, something of his capacity for fouling things up. We have learned something of his shrewd sense of indirection, his easy tolerance of disorder. These understandings and impressions come by osmosis, over a period of generations; it is an inheritance of observation and experience.

My own feeling, confirmed by travels throughout the South in recent years, is that the relationship of Southern white and Southern Negro is altering with remarkable speed. This change is not constant over the region as a whole. It is rapid in parts of Virginia, North Carolina, and Florida; slow in most of Alabama and nearly all of

Mississippi. But the current is in motion. It may be useful to try to explain why this is happening, and why I believe this tide holds such promise of tranquillity. It is because many Southerners, reared to a nonthinking acceptance of a certain way of life, abruptly and uncomfortably have begun to think about certain aspects of that way of life from the Negro's point of view. It is a point of view that never had quite occurred to them before.

"Massive Calamity"

It was not until after World War I that many of us began to look at these matters with a new and suddenly perceptive eye. Little by little, we are comprehending the injustice inherent in certain ancient customs. Where once we accepted segregation in public transportation as a simple way of life, now such a practice is widely viewed as simply absurd. In my own city of Richmond, whites and Negroes sit indifferently on the buses, where they please, and no one pays the slightest attention. Most of us were raised to the custom of segregated libraries. The Negroes had branches of their own. Now the idea of a segregated library seems grotesque. In the same fashion, we have become accustomed to Negro police, Negro firemen, Negro clerks, Negro operators of construction equipment. And all of these changes have been grafted solidly onto a body of some three hundred years of history.

At the same time we have also comprehended what so many of our liberal friends refuse to comprehend, that in terms of the whites' social and cultural values, the Negro people, as a people, are in truth today not equal to the white people, as a people, and that overnight "integration," predicated upon imagined equality, is the cruelest illusion of all. In most rural Southern communities, massive integration of public schools would mean massive calamity. Where white persons constitute a political minority, as they do in 140 Southern counties, the wholesale extension of the franchise overnight would mean disruption of order. No law, and no court decree, in and of itself, can produce "equality." Excluding all arguments about heredity, nothing but time can produce the home environments that contribute to excellence in education. Today's Negroes are three hundred years from African jungles; but the whites, by God's grace, are two thousand years from Greece and Rome.

This is, of course, the American dilemma, and the South's dilemma. As Garry Wills has remarked in *National Review*, the problem is to acquire the patience "of the bewildered parent who recognizes himself in the odd behavior of his growing son, and not expect invariably adult composure from people only now being allowed to exercise some of their legitimate adult rights." The point is that, by and large, the Negro has not reached social adulthood. We compound error by pretending that he has; and we should understand that the process of growth and maturity cannot be hurried by artificial stimulations.

The Color of Money

My second premise, in believing that the South will find a *modus vivendi* sooner than Harlem, stems from the economic opportunities that will be available to the Southern Negro. Profit will open doors for him that custom has kept closed.

If we of the South can resolve these questions of race, *and we can*, there is no visible limit to the region's economic potential. We are like an underdeveloped nation just awakening to the prospects of tourism, research and development, light manufacturing, the new technology. We have uncrowded cities, inviting land, congenial people, a productive climate. In most of its urban areas, the South is growing far more rapidly than other parts of the country; and while there is much "guv'mint money" in this growth, there is much venture capital also.

The Negro is bound to share in all this. Every year his educational opportunities improve. Twenty years ago, it was fair to say that all Negro schools were unequal. Today some Negro schools remain so, but, at least in terms of physical facilities, a great many Negro schools are superior to their white counterparts. White and Negro teaching staffs are equally certified in terms of academic degrees. They are equally paid. And one step at a time, without the racist lunacies of "busing," desegregation of schools advances cautiously across the South. We understand more and more that, in the strange new world of cybernetics and control machines, Negro youths must be educated to find productive employment. The alternative is the loss of buying power and the expense of a welfare roll.

In 1940, the median income of the American Negro, amounting to less than $500, was about 41 per cent of the white median. By 1960, the Negro's median income had grown to $3,075, six times the 1940 figure and amounting to some 60 per cent of the white. There have been still further improvements since then. Across the South a new Negro middle class is evolving, buying homes, furnishings, automobiles, appliances. A new generation of white merchants is interested not in the color of the Negro's skin, but in the color of his money.

This is not cupidity or venality or exploitation; it is becoming good business. The more money the Negro has to spend, the more he will find restaurants, stores, and home-builders competing for his trade. The 1960 census reported 97,000 Negro home-owners in Alabama, 90,000 in Georgia, 79,000 in Mississippi. They were part of nearly two million Negro home-owners in the country as a whole. The next census will find these figures notably enlarged, and some of the most encouraging increases will be in the South.

New Tenants

The foundations of history and the forces of economics will be accompanied by a third factor working in the Negro's behalf. He is coming into his own, as a voter, at the very time the South is experiencing political upheaval. Politically, the Negro never used to matter in the South. If he voted at all, he voted Republican. Even in the largest cities, until quite recently, white candidates for public office seldom bothered to campaign in Negro wards. And there were no Negro candidates.

It is astonishing—and unsettling—to note how swiftly this has changed. Democratic primaries, which once were "tantamount to election," are not nearly so tantamount now. A genuine two-party system is being developed. With the abolition of the poll tax in federal elections, Negroes are voting by the thousands. The Southern Regional Council has estimated that 2,250,000 Negroes in the old Confederacy states were registered to vote in 1964. These colored legions are voting in disciplined and cohesive blocs. Sometimes they are electing candidates of their own race. In the confusion of Democratic and Republican contests, they move by tentative steps toward an occasional balance of power. There is substance in the Negroes' assertion that Lyndon Johnson carried such states as Virginia, North Carolina, and Florida only with their votes.

This new political power is principally an urban phenomenon, but the South gets more urban all the time. Some strangely unfamiliar alliances are forming between liberal Democrats and the new Negro voters. A great many conservative Democrats in public office have begun to think seriously about an outright shift in party affiliation. Senator Strom Thurmond of South Carolina made this dramatic switch in 1964. Others inevitably will follow his lead. It is not at all improbable that the next ten or fifteen years will see a South as solidly Republican, in certain urban areas, as it once was solidly Democratic. The conservative-oriented majority will have abandoned the house of its fathers to some new tenants. The Negro is moving in, as voter, candidate, and office holder.

Those of us who have lived all our lives in the South as members of the "dominant white majority"—as conservatives, as segregationists—find it an amazing time. Change comes at a pace that may seem slow to others, but swift indeed to us. Within the professional communities and within many business communities also, Negro doctors, educators, bankers, insurance men, real-estate dealers are gaining admission to the ordinary intercourse of ordinary men. We move beyond the old era of stilted "biracial committees," where everyone was on his best behavior, guarded as ambassadors at tea; and very gradually we explore new relationships. It is a process of infinitely slow discovery; we grope with great caution, often out of sight of one another, and now and again we retreat from offensive

Negro militancy, or find a path closed by hated federal coercion, or see tranquillity destroyed by some idiot who bombs a Negro church. But we tend to find more clearings than we used to.

A Certain Receptivity

The process is helped in the South, ironically enough, by the very migration that has contributed to the North's problems. It is reasonable to surmise that the Negroes who have left the South are the dissatisfied, the restless, the ambitious, the militant. As they have moved out, they have left behind a relatively larger proportion of the contented, the indifferent, the nonmilitant. There remain in the South many aggressive Negro leaders, but there are not quite so many aggressive followers, hot for revolution, ready to lie down in streets and throw bottles at the cops. Southern Negro communities, for all the inmigration from farms, are growing more stable. On both sides of the racial barrier good manners survive.

Doubtless many Negro families who have left the South will find happiness in Northern cities—better income, better education, and community acceptance. The Lord be with them. But my guess is that the outflow of Southern Negroes will taper off in coming years, and the next census may even show signs of an occasional return of disillusioned expatriates to the land of their birth. They will find no paradise—not many persons ever do—but they will find in the emerging South a certain receptivity and maturity that promise for both races a better time ahead.

VII

W. J. Cash after a Quarter Century

◆

by EDWIN M. YODER

In February 1941 Wilbur J. Cash, an erratic North Carolina journalist who wrote editorials for the Charlotte *News*, published *The Mind of the South*, a volume instantly recognized by students of regional analysis as a classic.* Subsequent works on the same subject have almost been footnotes.

Until Cash really showed how crucial the historical dimension is to an understanding of the South, its eccentricities were inflated by admirers, scoffed at by reformers. Profiles of the region ran to one of two unhelpful extremes. One saw either a bizarre wonderland full of hotheaded "Southrons," or a sterile waste from which ´social scientists had removed the people, whose vagaries were simply matters of poverty, pellagra, and poll taxes. In the first, the past was distorted out of all recognition; in the second, it was ignored. *The Mind of the South* recalls Carl Becker's observation about Jefferson: he felt with his mind as some think with their hearts. Cash was not the first to explore the Southern mind—"a fairly definite mental pattern, associ-

* But the author did not stay around to collect laurels. Taking a Guggenheim grant, Cash, then forty-one, went to Mexico City. There, a few weeks later, his nerves apparently shot, he hanged himself in a hotel.

ated with a fairly definite social pattern," as he defined it. But his map remains the most plausible we have.

To understand *The Mind of the South*, its muffled bitterness, its permanent value and fascination, one must understand Cash's mind —and its obsession with cotton. He was born and spent his boyhood in a cotton mill town, Gaffney, South Carolina, where his father operated a company store. When he later composed a rather self-consciously romantic autobiography for H. L. Mencken's *American Mercury*, where his early essays appeared, Cash recalled that "the keening of the five o'clock whistles . . . drilled me in sorrow."

Those whistles, beckoning the millworkers—the "lintheads"—to the spindles were the characteristic sound of Cash's South. When he thought of cotton, it was not of wide fields but of an altogether different and drearier picture: "company houses," clouds of lint, and lung diseases. Cash saw a Hardyesque pathos in his early life. He was a sensitive boy, nearsighted from secret reading, restless, as he wrote Mencken, at "the Baptist preacher's too graphic account of the Second Coming"; he expected an apocalypse every sunset. He was out of sympathy with the brutalities of his childhood setting and with the economic nexus that brought them about. When he saw a rich cotton-mill manager passing down the street, he felt that some ingredient in the traditional myth of a sympathetic and gracious South was being betrayed. Hadn't the "Confederate captains," as the old gentry are called in his book, built the cotton mills for humanitarian reasons, to salvage the sinking tenant farmer from economic ruin? And what was one to think of the hopeless mental primitiveness of a culture, all too typically represented by the fulminations of the parson—a civilization which had not even begun to come to terms with Darwin and Freud?

A Deeper Scrutiny

From this difficulty at reconciling myth and fact there sprung, initially, a lively if unoriginal iconoclasm. Like all enterprising young journalists of his day, Cash wrote in the manner of Mencken. It was in fairly good imitation Mencken that he fired his initial salvos in the pages of the *Mercury* at his childhood villains. But as Cash matured, so did his tactics. Reading back now over the bombastic essays he published in the *Mercury* in the late 1920s, one might suppose that in time he grew tired of firing point-blank and began to contemplate a more subtle strategy for solving the regional anomalies. He stopped writing for Mencken and began to look deep into the political, psychological, and social evolution that had set the South apart. This scrutiny, lasting for twelve years, was to culminate in *The Mind of the South*.

That mind, Cash came to believe, is primarily a frontier mind, bearing the marks of a rough and ready beginning. It is, he writes, "a tree with many age rings . . . but with its taproot in the Old South." The period of its formation was 1830–1860, the setting the South beyond the coastal settlements in the back country, "the man at the center" the upland cotton planter. In a dense but powerful style, Cash imagines how this prototype of the Southerner scrambled precariously to imitate the coastal Old Regime whose more genteel ways he both hated and envied. The upland Southerner's struggle to assimilate the way of life of the tidewater "Virginians" covered little more than a generation before the Civil War. This process was never concluded, and it is not surprising that Cash could write of the manner of this kind of Southerner: "It was ultimately not an emanation from the proper substance of the men who wore it, but only a fine garment put on from the outside."

Furthermore, Cash concluded, the characteristic sectionalism of that frontier mind was a defense—a reaction. Before the war, the Abolitionist assailed the immortality of slavery. After the war, the Carpetbagger and Radical so plundered the South, always with high moralizing, that the Southerner was driven to assume that he *was* "different," if only in self-defense.

The ruin of the economic system was so complete that the frontier was reopened. Poverty and social ferment—"the frontier the Yankee made," Cash calls it—returned. So this new man who in antebellum days had never fully defined himself was once again cut adrift in a world that rewarded his cunning and calculation—and sometimes violence—at the same time that he espoused a romantic view of the past. The Southerner imagined, in a setting dulled by ruin, a never-never land in which his unrealized aspirations to ease, grandeur, and graciousness had once been realized after all. That this myth was false was beside the point; it became a vital factor in his mentality. Cash thought he had found the key to an enigmatic culture that pretended to mellowness, but could be crass; that pretended to chivalry, but could be savage; whose legendary hospitality consorted with political demagogy, violence, anti-intellectualism, and a funda-mentalism on basic principles which found an occasional outlet in what Cash calls "the savage ideal"—the ideal of total conformity.

Tied to the Land

At several points the historian must, after twenty-five years, quarrel with Cash. Revisionist historians of the Reconstruction period—among whom a Southerner, Francis Butler Simkins, is notable—now tell us there was more to that period than Yankee piracy and the brutal economic imperialism of Cash's "tariff gang." Other critics have found Cash's treatment of Southern religion superficial—"the trivial booing . . . we heard so much in the 1920s," says Donald Davidson.

These reinterpretations aside, has the essential behavior of the South as Cash described it changed radically in the last quarter-century? On the whole the answer seems to me No—notwithstanding obvious economic and social modifications that are often heralded today, as in the 1890s, as constituting a "New" South. In truth "the mind of the South" seems today to defy the impersonal forces. When you put aside the spread of television sets, the advent of jet air travel, the larger cash incomes (all consistent with national developments), you are left with a mental pattern familiar to Cash: the race picture, though increasingly subject to federal legal pressure, is mostly as Cash saw it—status politics still intact. The South is still given, more than any single identifiable region, to unholy repressions of wrong thinking. Its economy, though diversified, though emancipated from the cotton mills on which Cash obsessively spent almost a third of his book, has yet to transform the South into a truly industrial or urban society. Its habits are still tied to the land.

But let me specify.

No sane person denies today, North and South, the existence of a second American revolution in race relations. But it is easy amidst the one way flow of legal and legislative mandates from Washington to lose sight of those durable Southern habits which, being more subtle than most critics suppose, defy political command. Race preoccupies the South today as much as (if not more than) when Cash wrote in 1941. In flippant moments, Southern newspaper editors still call it "Topic A," a label rarely applied without a weary sigh that such a preoccupation should stand, virtually immovable, between the South and its dream of modernity.

Cash's analysis of the "proto-Dorian convention" still applies:

> If the plantation had introduced distinctions of wealth and rank among the men of the old backcountry, and, in doing so, had perhaps offended against the ego of the common white, it had also . . . introduced that other vastly ego-warming and ego-expanding distinction between the white man and the black. Robbing him and degrading him in so many ways, it yet, by a singular irony, had simultaneously elevated this common white to a position comparable to that of, say, the Doric knight of ancient Sparta. Not only was he not exploited directly, he was himself made by extension a member of the dominant class—was lodged solidly on a tremendous superiority, which . . . he could never publicly lose. Come what might, he would always be a white man. And before that vast and capacious distinction, all others were foreshortened, dwarfed, and all but obliterated.
>
> The grand outcome was the almost complete disappearance of economic and social focus on the part of the masses. . . .

Even today, the enduring presence of Negroes in large numbers forbids, except in the most tranquil moments of truce between Washington and Birmingham or Jackson or Albany, Georgia, the practice of genuine interest politics. For whatever the South has chosen to accept in the way of racial practices, it has not yet accepted in any state that entire division of political opinion along lines of natural economic interest that could make Negro votes decisive and thus raise what Francis Butler Simkins calls "the bête noire of Southern politics—the election of Negroes in considerable numbers."

The Cry of Status Politics

Governor Wallace, for instance, understands the Cash analysis. Though by the Bilbo-Vardaman standard the Governor of Alabama is an elegant refinement, his political appeal rests on a canny insight into the "proto-Dorian" standing of the Southern poor white—the fixture that he must never be threatened with submergence below the mass of Negroes in the social and political heap. Naturally, the new Southern demagogue has updated his vocabulary. He is much given to denunciation of foreign devils. He rarely uses the word "nigger" in public. But when he attacks parts of the federal Civil Rights Bill for threatening hiring and firing rights of the longshoremen's local in Mobile, his listeners recognize, however cleverly sugared for distant consumption, the cry of status politics.

To say that Cash's analysis of race politics is still pertinent is not to say, of course, that it will always remain so. The present stage may be transitional. Certainly Southern politics of even the most die-hard kind must come to terms with Negro voters newly enfranchised by the registration sanctions of the civil-rights laws. And their votes will carry more weight if the Supreme Court persists in its current attack on malapportionment. Only another spell of fatigue such as overcame the national political consensus by 1877 can postpone this showdown; and Senator Goldwater's failure to find and exploit the rumored "white backlash" in the 1964 election makes such a prospect dim. Still, it is well to remember that the Goldwater-Wallace axis did exist, however weakly, and that it formed a precedent of sorts in American politics.

If an absence of radical change in race relations is discernible, the same is true of what Cash called "the savage ideal"—"that ideal whereunder dissent and variety are completely suppressed and men become, for all their attitudes, professions, and actions, virtual replicas of one another." The South's ideals of tolerance are today hardly those of John Stuart Mill, or even of Thomas Jefferson. Doctrinal diversity, questions about the basic assumptions of the social and economic system, are largely confined to the intelligentsia. Cash was guilty of a great exaggeration, of course, when he likened the savage ideal of his day to the mad authoritarianism then in vogue among European dictators. After all, the key word is *ideal*. When repression-minded Southern legislators curtail freedoms of speech, organization, teaching, or movement, it is usually, so they say in all good faith, for the sake of a higher good. The Southern vigilante strikes out at threatening scientific or social ideas with a Rotarian highmindedness and sobriety that has little in common with Hitlerian nihilism. When fundamentalist parsons throng (they recently did) to meetings of the Texas State Textbook Committee, hoping to put Darwin in his place; or when North Carolina legislators shut state college campuses to pleaders of the Fifth Amendment, as they did in June 1963; when a professor is given walking papers in the Deep South; when these things occur they are usually said to protect school children against dangerous thoughts. Even today the apologists for a closed society in parts of the South fall back on a premise—sometimes unspoken—that the Southerner cannot analyze an idea. And it is ironic evidence of the continued pertinence of Cash that in making this observation himself, he even borrowed on that arch-scold of the South, Henry Adams.

Limits on Economic Change

In the Southern economy, change is most obvious to the casual eye and durability is difficult to spot. Here I think Cash himself was partially deceived. If *The Mind of the South* has a major flaw, it is a naïve faith in the power of specific changes in the Southern economy to revolutionize social, political, and mental patterns. To say this is not to scoff condescendingly; John Kenneth Galbraith was hardly the first to tell us that Productivity is, for Americans, a sovereign index to society. What is strange is that Cash, having for some two hundred pages sought to show the basic indestructibility of the Southern mind under a barrage of economic changes, should then profess to believe that the mere unionization of cotton millworkers would herald a new day. Of course we have heard of the "New South" for generations; and for every generation, the meaning of the vision differs slightly, though it usually has much to do with industrialization or industrial sophistication. It is typical that in Robert Lerché's *The Uncertain South,* a recent study of Southern voting patterns in the House, the author ends an exhausting exercise in statistical gymnastics with the old conclusion that industrialism and urbanism will end the "uncertainty."

Were it that simple, the South would long since, I think, have put up or shut up. The trouble with the industrial panacea is that it rests on too simple assumptions about what makes a society run. It is as tired as the anecdote Henry Grady used to tell about the Georgia funeral for which that underindustrialized state supplied only the corpse and the hole in the ground.

Were Cash writing today, what might startle him is that the wholesale unionization he saw in prospect never came. It was beaten by right-to-work laws, by a plenitude of "Anglo-Saxon labor" out of the hills, and by high-priced legal talent. But an even more important deterrent was that fierce individualism, that aversion to regimentation, that could be noted—as Cash recorded—in the behavior of the Boys in Gray, who elected their officers and took unkindly to sharp command. Why Cash, having sketched "one of the world's most remarkable individualists" in the person of the Southern cracker, nonetheless believed that he could become a dutiful and disciplined modern labor unionist I cannot say. But he did so believe.

Even more to the point are the observations of Professor William H. Nicholls of Vanderbilt, recently president of the Southern Economic Association. Nicholls speaks not only as a devotee of industrial progress but as one whose firsthand inspection of the effect (or non-effect) of foreign aid has given him insights into the riddle of the Southern economy. The more he has seen of the infusion of capital into economically "backward" lands, he says, the more he has been convinced that profound economic change does *not* produce social change—but rather vice versa. Regional "progress" will not come about so long as the South remains bound by "agrarian values, the rigidity . . . of the social structure, the weakness of social responsibility, and the conformity of thought and behavior"—just the catalogue of qualities which advocates of the various "New Souths" have usually sought to relieve by industrialization.

"No Wonder You Have to Come Away"

The picture I draw, then, assessing Cash's book twenty-five years after, is one in which stability outweighs change. Oddly, this state of affairs seems to me reinforced, and in a way made respectable, by a succession of writers and professors who with genuine critical detachment tell Southerners—and outsiders—that it is not so bad to be different. Reviewing Cash's book for *The Nation* in 1941, James Orrick noted: "What makes the mind of the South different is that it thinks it is." And while C. Vann Woodward's conception of the difference in his superb book, *The Burden of Southern History*, departs drastically from that of neo-Ku Kluxers, everyone joins in the refrain of "Vive la différence."

The Southerner's attachment to this "difference" in the Southern mind has two sides—one defensible in down-to-earth terms, the other admittedly difficult to reduce to sociological paraphrase. In 1941, Cash could conclude by saying of the region: "Proud, brave, honorable by its lights, courteous, personally generous, loyal, swift to act, often too swift, but signally effective, sometimes terrible, in its action—such was the South at its best. And such at its best it remains today, despite the great falling away in some of its virtues."

On the practical side, by way of apology for the Southern mind, it is hard to better Vann Woodward's formulation: that in a nation conditioned by a happy history to victory, plenty, and a consequent optimism about the susceptibility of human affairs to beneficial innovation, the South has been a tempering force. Knowing defeat, scarcity, and failure to root out an intractable social evil the South has a sense of common destiny with the larger world (which has shared defeat, poverty, and tragedy). This departure from the unmarred triumph of the national experience has surely helped the South supply more than its quota of creative statesmen on the world scene, from Wilson and Hull to Johnson and Rusk and Fulbright. And it is the sense of abiding tragedy that has enriched Southern fiction and made it pre-eminent.

The mystical side is best approached through Southern literature, where one encounters directly the fetishes of family, physical place, and tradition that are so important, or were, in the Southern mind. The curious difficulty of communication here is beautifully illustrated in Faulkner's great novel, *Absalom, Absalom!*, when Quentin Compson pauses from his obsessive narrative of the rise and fall of the Sutpen dynasty, and is blandly interrupted by Shreve, his Canadian roommate at Harvard:

"So he just wanted a grandson," Shreve said. "That was all he was after. Jesus, the South is fine, isn't it. It's better than the theatre, isn't it. It's better than Ben Hur, isn't it. No wonder you have to come away now and then. . . ."

In a highly commercialized and mobile society that has replaced ties of blood and household with abstractions of a fairly impersonal sort, one is apt to confront these bloody and tortured Southern iliads just as Shreve does. They will seem out of date to some, melodramatic and perverse to many, and so, I suppose, they will remain.

A Tacit Alliance?

Perhaps, then, Cash defined the "difference" beyond improvement—and hence gave us the key to his own continued pertinence—when he chose his title. Being Southern *is* a state of mind—a condition of chronic introspection reaching its highest imaginative pitch, perhaps, in Faulkner's reflective heroes like the Reverend Gail Hightower and Isaac McCaslin.

Cash himself is a case of this. He did much by writing his book to enhance regional self-consciousness as an ideal per se—and so reinforced the tacit alliance that reaches down from the rarefied meditations of professors, authors, and journalists to the inchoate consciousness of the leather-jacketed hot-rodder who sports a Confederate battle flag on the rear bumper. These improbable allies differ in almost everything except the proposition that the South is and should remain "a nation within a nation" and so much the better so.

Naturally, I am not suggesting a continuity of motives or objectives here, let alone a dark conspiracy. It is a fair guess that the fine points of the Southern mystique are of more interest to Cash's successors than to the "hell of a fellow" (to borrow a good Cashian phrase) who puts the Stars and Bars in the same decorative class with foxtails, Spanish moss, jeweled mudguards, and twin exhaust pipes. And it is an open question how much the meditations of the regional intellectuals and creative writers sustain this unholy alliance.

There is, however, little doubt that if the South lacked working mythologists to go on holding up a mirror to "the mind of the South" this mind would vanish as a distinctive study in self-consciousness. But I confess my own relief that Cash's successors remain at work. It is not only that human variety is instructive, if not always pleasing to the moral sense. Self-knowledge remains, one assumes, the virtue it was for the ancients—not only for the South itself but for a nation which too often supposes in pride and vanity that it will eventually remake mankind in its own definitive image.

VIII

A Vanishing Era

♦

by WHITNEY M. YOUNG, JR.

The era of the emasculated Southern Negro male is vanishing.

I clearly recall experiences in my childhood which occurred because white people could not dare think of the Negro male as a man. It was my mother who took me back to the store when the suit didn't fit properly, and who succeeded in getting it altered without charge. For my father to object to a white clerk might have marked him as "uppity" and ruined his life's work. Even though he was president of the Lincoln Ridge School near Louisville, now a state-supported Negro boarding school, he had to resort to the cunning of a character out of William Dean Howells when the question of Negro manhood was involved.

Father would set out each semester to recruit Negro youth from the rural plantations for his school. The plantation owners could not readily see a potential farmhand becoming a literate, self-sufficient citizen. The first thing Father did riding into town in his old buggy was to find out who the colored man was—the one Negro in the place oblivious to intimidation and having no fear for his safety. This person—all the better if he was a hulking behemoth of a man—traveled around the country with my father to give weight to his pleas for school recruits. All this was because the Southern ethos at the time tended to keep the Negro male down and the Negro family as consciously disorganized after slavery as it was deliberately destroyed during slavery.

No such subterfuge would be required by my father today. Recent reports of the gains by Negro men in the professions and skilled trades in Southern cities have been encouraging. The gallant young men of the Southern civil-rights movement have broken with the custom of the nonexistent black man and will go on to strengthen Negro family life.

More and more, these young men are remaining in the South. When I graduated from college in 1941, there was no graduate school in Kentucky which I could attend. Like so many others, I left Kentucky, and I have never returned except for visits. In my early adult years, the South was still chasing out its best leadership—black men who could not learn and white men who could not live under such a system. Now that many state and privately supported universities have been opened, I foresee a growing body of Negro intellectuals who will choose to remain, and who will elect to make their homes in the cosmopolitan urban centers where racial barriers in public places and in employment are dropping.

I recall, as a young man, a motel on Highway 41 between Atlanta and Nashville; in front was a sign advertising "Cold Beer" for whites and "Cool Beer" for Negroes. These and other less humorous proclamations to servitude never allowed us to forget our inferior status. In my college days, when I worked washing dishes for Louisville's Seelbach Hotel, now the Sheraton, I could only ride the service elevator. Today, when the Urban League holds a convention there, I am offered the presidential suite in the same hotel; my brothers and I are treated with every respect. The disappearance of the many outward signs of segregation prompted by the Civil Rights Act of 1964 is certain to encourage more Southern Negroes to remain Southerners. If most of the South has a farther way to go than the rest of America, I believe it is at least going there quicker.

IX

Why I Returned

◆

by ARNA BONTEMPS

The last time I visited Louisiana, the house in which I was born was freshly painted. To my surprise, it seemed almost attractive. The present occupants, I learned, were a Negro minister and his family. Why I expected the place to be run down and the neighborhood decayed is not clear, but somewhere in my subconscious the notion that rapid deterioration was inevitable where Negroes live had been planted and allowed to grow. Moreover, familiar as I am with the gloomier aspects of living Jim Crow, this assumption did not appall me. I could reject the snide inferences. Seeing my birthplace again, however, after many years, I felt apologetic on other grounds.

Mine had not been a varmint-infested childhood so often the hallmark of Negro American autobiography. My parents and grandparents had been well-fed, well-clothed, and well-housed, although in my earliest recollections of the corner at Ninth and Winn in Alexandria both streets were rutted and sloppy. On Winn there was an abominable ditch where water settled for weeks at a time. I can remember Crazy George, the town idiot, following a flock of geese with the bough of a tree in his hand, standing in slush while the geese paddled about or probed into the muck. So fascinated was I, in fact, I did not hear my grandmother calling from the kitchen door. It was after I felt her hand on my shoulder shaking me out of my daydream that I said something that made her laugh. "You called me Arna," I protested, when she insisted on knowing why I had not answered. "My name is George." But I became Arna for the rest of her years.

I had already become aware of nicknames among the people we regarded as members of the family. Teel, Mousie, Buddy, Pinkie, Yaya, Mat, and Pig all had other names which one heard occasionally. I got the impression that to be loved intensely one needed a nick- name. I was glad my grandmother, whose love mattered so much, had found one she liked for me.

As I recall, my hand was in my grandmother's a good part of the time. If we were not standing outside the picket gate waiting for my young uncles to come home from school, we were under the tree in the front yard picking up pecans after one of the boys had climbed up and shaken the branches. If we were not decorating a backyard bush with eggshells, we were driving in our buggy across the bridge to Pineville on the other side of the Red River.

This idyll came to a sudden, senseless end at a time when every-thing about it seemed flawless. One afternoon my mother and her several sisters had come out of their sewing room with thimbles still on their fingers, needles and thread stuck to their tiny aprons, to fill their pockets with pecans. Next, it seemed, we were at the railroad station catching a train to California, my mother, sister, and I, with a young woman named Susy.

The story behind it, I learned, concerned my father. When he was not away working at brick or stone construction, other things occu-pied his time. He had come from a family of builders. His oldest brother had married into the Metoyer family on Cane River, de-scendants of the free Negroes who were the original builders of the famous Melrose plantation mansion. Another brother older than my father went down to New Orleans, where his daughter married one of the prominent jazzmen. My father was a bandman himself and, when he was not working too far away, the chances were he would be blowing his horn under the direction of Claiborne Williams, whose passion for band music awakened the impulse that worked its way up the river and helped to quicken American popular music.

My father was one of those dark Negroes with "good" hair, meaning almost straight. This did not bother anybody in Avoyelles Parish, where the type was common and "broken French" accents expected, but later in California people who had traveled in the Far East wondered if he were not a Ceylonese or something equally exotic. In Alexandria his looks, good clothes, and hauteur were something of a disadvantage in the first decade of this century.

He was walking on Lee Street one night when two white men wavered out of a saloon and blocked his path. One of them muttered, "Let's walk over the big nigger." My father was capable of fury, and he might have reasoned differently at another time, but that night he calmly stepped aside, allowing the pair to have the walk to themselves. The decision he made as he walked on home changed everything for all of us.

II

My first clear memory of my father as a person is of him waiting for us outside the Southern Pacific Depot in Los Angeles. He was shy about showing emotion, and he greeted us quickly on our arrival and let us know this was the place he had chosen for us to end our journey. We had tickets to San Francisco and were prepared to continue beyond if necessary.

We moved into a house in a neighborhood where we were the only colored family. The people next door and up and down the block were friendly and talkative, the weather was perfect, there wasn't a mud puddle anywhere, and my mother seemed to float about on the clean air. When my grandmother and a host of others followed us to this refreshing new country, I began to pick up comment about the place we had left, comment which had been withheld from me while we were still in Louisiana.

They talked mainly about my grandmother's younger brother, nicknamed Buddy. I could not remember seeing him in Louisiana, and I now learned he had been down at the Keeley Institute in New

Orleans taking a cure for alcoholism. A framed portrait of Uncle Buddy was placed in my grandmother's living room in California, a young mulatto dandy in elegant cravat and jeweled stickpin. All the talk about him gave me an impression of style, grace, éclat.

That impression vanished a few years later, however, when we gathered to wait for him in my grandmother's house; he entered wearing a detachable collar without a tie. His clothes did not fit. They had been slept in for nearly a week on the train. His shoes had come unlaced. His face was pockmarked. Nothing resembled the picture in the living room.

Two things redeemed the occasion, however. He opened his make-shift luggage and brought out jars of syrup, bags of candy my grand-mother had said in her letters that she missed, pecans, and filé for making gumbo. He had stuffed his suitcase with these instead of clothes; he had not brought an overcoat or a change of underwear. As we ate the sweets, he began to talk. He was not trying to impress or even entertain us. He was just telling how things were down home, how he had not taken a drink or been locked up since he came back from Keeley the last time, how the family of his employer and bene-factor had been scattered or died, how the school-teacher friend of the family was getting along, how high the Red River had risen along the levee, and such things.

Someone mentioned his white employer's daughter. A rumor per-sisted that Buddy had once had a dangerous crush on her. This, I took it, had to be back in the days when the picture in the living room was made, but the dim suggestion of interracial romance had an air of unreality. It was all mostly gossip, he commented, with only a shadow of a smile. Never had been much to it, and it was too long ago to talk about now. He did acknowledge, significantly, I thought, that his boss's daughter had been responsible for his enjoy-ment of poetry and fiction and had taught him perhaps a thousand songs, but neither of these circumstances had undermined his life-long employment in her father's bakery, where his specialty was fancy cakes. Buddy had never married. Neither had the girl.

When my mother became ill, a year or so after Buddy's arrival, we went to live with my grandmother in the country for a time. Buddy was there. He had acquired a rusticity wholly foreign to his upbringing. He had never before worked out of doors. Smoking a corncob pipe and wearing oversized clothes provided by my uncles, he resembled a scarecrow in the garden, but the dry air and the smell of green vegetables seemed to be good for him. I promptly became his companion and confidant in the corn rows.

At mealtime we were occasionally joined by my father, home from his bricklaying. The two men eyed each other with suspicion, but they did not quarrel immediately. Mostly they reminisced about Louisiana. My father would say, "Sometimes I miss all that. If I was just thinking about myself, I might want to go back and try it again. But I've got the children to think about—their education."

"Folks talk a lot about California," Buddy would reply thoughtfully, "but I'd a heap rather be down home than here, if it wasn't for the *conditions*."

Obviously their remarks made sense to each other, but they left me with a deepening question. Why was this exchange repeated after so many of their conversations? What was it that made the South—excusing what Buddy called the *conditions*—so appealing for them?

There was less accord between them in the attitudes they revealed when each of the men talked to me privately. My father respected Buddy's ability to quote the whole of Thomas Hood's "The Vision of Eugene Aram," praised his reading and spelling ability, but he was concerned, almost troubled, about the possibility of my adopting the old derelict as an example. He was horrified by Buddy's casual and frequent use of the word *nigger*. Buddy even forgot and used it in the presence of white people once or twice that year, and was soundly criticized for it. Buddy's new friends, moreover, were sometimes below the level of polite respect. They were not bad people. They were what my father described as don't-care folk. To top it all, Buddy was still crazy about the minstrel shows and minstrel talk that had been the joy of his young manhood. He loved dialect stories, preacher stories, ghost stories, slave and master stories. He half-believed in signs and charms and mumbo-jumbo, and he believed wholeheartedly in ghosts.

I took it that my father was still endeavoring to counter Buddy's baneful influence when he sent me away to a white boarding school during my high school years, after my mother had died. "Now don't go up there acting colored," he cautioned. I believe I carried out his wish. He sometimes threatened to pull me out of school and let me scuffle for myself the minute I fell short in any one of several ways he indicated. Before I finished college, I had begun to feel that in some large and important areas I was being miseducated, and that perhaps I should have rebelled.

III

How dare anyone, parent, schoolteacher, or merely literary critic, tell me not to act *colored*? White people have been enjoying the privilege of acting like Negroes for more than a hundred years. The minstrel show, their most popular form of entertainment in America for a whole generation, simply epitomized, while it exaggerated, this privilege. Today nearly everyone who goes on a dance floor starts acting colored immediately, and this had been going on since the cakewalk was picked up from Negroes and became the rage. Why should I be ashamed of such influences? In popular music, as in the music of religious fervor, there is a style that is unmistakable, and its origin is certainly no mystery. On the playing field a Willie Mays could be detected by the way he catches a ball, even if his face were hidden. Should the way some Negroes walk be changed or emulated? Sometimes it is possible to tell whether or not a cook is a Negro without going into the kitchen. How about this?

In their opposing attitudes toward roots my father and my great uncle made me aware of a conflict in which every educated American Negro, and some who are not educated, must somehow take sides. By implication at least, one group advocates embracing the riches of the folk heritage; their opposites demand a clean break with the past and all it represents. Had I not gone home summers and hobnobbed with Negroes, I would have finished college without knowing that any Negro other than Paul Laurence Dunbar ever wrote a poem. I would have come out imagining that the story of the Negro could be told in two short paragraphs: a statement about jungle people in

Africa and an equally brief account of the slavery issue in American history.

So what did one do after concluding that for him a break with the past and the shedding of his Negro-ness were not only impossible but unthinkable? First, perhaps, like myself, he went to New York in the twenties, met young Negro writers and intellectuals who were similarly searching, learned poems like Claude McKay's "Harlem Dancer" and Jean Toomer's "Song of the Son," and started writing and publishing things in this vein himself.

My first book was published just after the Depression struck. Buddy was in it, conspicuously, and I sent him a copy, which I imagine he read. In any case, he took the occasion to celebrate. Returning from an evening with his don't-care friends, he wavered along the highway and was hit and killed by an automobile. He was sixty-seven, I believe.

Alfred Harcourt, Sr., was my publisher. When he invited me to the office, I found that he was also to be my editor. He explained with a smile that he was back on the job doing editorial work because of the hard times. I soon found out what he meant. Book business appeared to be as bad as every other kind, and the lively and talented young people I had met in Harlem were scurrying to whatever brier patches they could find. I found one in Alabama.

It was the best of times and the worst of times to run to that state for refuge. Best, because the summer air was so laden with honeysuckle and spiraea it almost drugged the senses at night. I have occasionally returned since then but never at a time when the green of trees, of countryside, or even of swamps seemed so wanton. While paying jobs were harder to find here than in New York, indeed scarcely existed, one did not see evidences of hunger. Negro girls worked in kitchens not for wages but for the toting privilege— permission to take home leftovers.

The men and boys rediscovered woods and swamps and streams with which their ancestors had been intimate a century earlier, and about which their grandparents still talked wistfully. The living critters still abounded. They were as wild and numerous as anybody had ever dreamed, some small, some edible, some monstrous. I made friends with these people and went with them on possum hunts, and I was astonished to learn how much game they could bring home without gunpowder, which they did not have. When the possum was treed by the dogs, a small boy went up and shook him off the limb, and the bigger fellows finished him with sticks. Nets and traps would do for birds and fish. Cottontail rabbits driven into a clearing were actually run down and caught by barefoot boys.

Such carryings-on amused them while it delighted their palates. It also took their minds off the hard times, and they were ready for church when Sunday came. I followed them there, too, and soon began to understand why they enjoyed it so much. The preaching called to mind James Weldon Johnson's "The Creation" and "Go Down Death." The long-meter singing was from another world. The shouting was ecstasy itself. At a primitive Baptist foot washing I saw benchwalking for the first time, and it left me breathless. The young woman who rose from her seat and skimmed from the front of the church to the back, her wet feet lightly touching the tops of the pews, her eyes upward, could have astounded me no more had she walked on water. The members fluttered and wailed, rocked the church with their singing, accepted the miracle for what it was.

IV

It was also the worst times to be in northern Alabama. That was the year, 1931, of the nine Scottsboro boys and their trials in nearby Decatur. Instead of chasing possums at night and swimming in creeks in the daytime, this group of kids without jobs and nothing else to do had taken to riding empty boxcars. When they found themselves in a boxcar with two white girls wearing overalls and traveling the same way, they knew they were in bad trouble. The charge against them was rape, and the usual finding in Alabama, when a Negro man was so much as remotely suspected, was guilty; the usual penalty, death.

To relieve the tension, as we hoped, we drove to Athens one night and listened to a program of music by young people from Negro high schools and colleges in the area. A visitor arrived from Decatur during the intermission and reported shocking developments at the trial that day. One of the girls involved had given testimony about herself which reasonably should have taken the onus from the boys. It had only succeeded in infuriating the crowd around the courthouse. The rumor that reached Athens was that crowds were spilling along the highway, lurking in unseemly places, threatening to vent their anger. After the music was over, someone suggested nervously that those of us from around Huntsville leave at the same time, keep our cars close together as we drove home, be prepared to stand by, possibly help, if anyone met with mischief.

We readily agreed. Though the drive home was actually uneventful, the tension remained, and I began to take stock with a seriousness comparable to my father's when he stepped aside for the Saturday night bullies on Lee Street in Alexandria. I was younger than he had been when he made his move, but my family was already larger by one. Moreover, I had weathered a Northern as well as a Southern exposure. My education was different, and what I was reading in newspapers differed greatly from anything he could have found in the Alexandria *Town Talk* in the first decade of this century.

With Gandhi making world news in India while the Scottsboro case inflamed passions in Alabama and awakened consciences elsewhere, I thought I could sense something beginning to shape up, possibly something on a wide scale. As a matter of fact, I had already written a stanza foreshadowing the application of a nonviolent strategy to the Negro's efforts in the South:

> We are not come to wage a strife
> With swords upon this hill;
> It is not wise to waste the life
> Against a stubborn will.
> Yet would we die as some have done:
> Beating a way for the rising sun.

Even so, deliverance did not yet seem imminent, and it was becoming plain that an able-bodied young Negro with a healthy family could not continue to keep friends in that community if he sat around trifling with a typewriter on the shady side of his house when he should have been working or at least trying to raise something for the table. So we moved on to Chicago.

Crime seemed to be the principal occupation of the South Side at the time of our arrival. The openness of it so startled us we could scarcely believe what we saw. Twice our small apartment was burglarized. Nearly every week we witnessed a stickup, a purse-snatching, or something equally dismaying on the street. Once I saw two men get out of a car, enter one of those blinded shops around the corner from us, return dragging a resisting victim, slam him into the back seat of the car, and speed away. We had fled from the jungle of Alabama's Scottsboro era to the jungle of Chicago's crime-ridden South Side, and one was as terrifying as the other.

Despite literary encouragement, and the heartiness of a writing clan that adopted me and bolstered my courage, I never felt that I could settle permanently with my family in Chicago. I could not accept the ghetto, and ironclad residential restrictions against Negroes situated as we were made escape impossible, confining us to neighborhoods where we had to fly home each evening before darkness fell and honest people abandoned the streets to predators. Garbage was dumped in alleys around us. Police protection was regarded as a farce. Corruption was everywhere.

When I inquired about transfers for two of our children to integrated schools which were actually more accessible to our address, I was referred to a person not connected with the school system or the city government. He assured me he could arrange the transfers—at an outrageous price. This represented ways in which Negro leadership was operating in the community at that time and by which it had been reduced to impotence.

I did not consider exchanging this way of life for the institutionalized assault on Negro personality one encountered in the Alabama of the Scottsboro trials, but suddenly the campus of a Negro college I had twice visited in Tennessee began to seem attractive. A measure of isolation, a degree of security seemed possible there. If a refuge for the harassed Negro could be found anywhere in the 1930s and 1940s, it had to be in such a setting.

Fisk University, since its beginnings in surplus barracks provided by a general of the occupying army six months after the close of the Civil War, had always striven to exemplify racial concord. Integration started immediately with children of white teachers and continued till state laws forced segregation after the turn of the century. Even then, a mixed faculty was retained, together with a liberal environment, and these eventually won a truce from an outside community that gradually changed from hostility to indifference to acceptance and perhaps a certain pride. Its founders helped fight the battle for public schools in Nashville, and donated part of the college's property for this purpose. Its students first introduced Negro spirituals to the musical world. The college provided a setting for a continuing dialogue between scholars across barriers and brought to the city before 1943 a pioneering Institute of Race Relations and a Program of African Studies, both firsts in the region. When a nationally known scholar told me in Chicago that he found the atmosphere *yeasty*, I thought I understood what he meant.

We had made the move, and I had become the Librarian at Fisk when a series of train trips during World War II gave me an opportunity for reflections of another kind. I started making notes for an essay to be called "Thoughts in a Jim Crow Car." Before I could finish it, Supreme Court action removed the curtains in the railway diners, and the essay lost its point. While I had been examining my own feelings and trying to understand the need men have for customs like this, the pattern had altered. Compliance followed with what struck me, surprisingly, as an attitude of relief by all concerned. White passengers, some of whom I recognized by their positions in the public life of Nashville, who had been in a habit of maintaining a frozen silence until the train crossed the Ohio River, now nodded and began chatting with Negroes before the train left the Nashville station. I wanted to stand up and cheer. When the Army began to desegregate its units, I was sure I detected a fatal weakness in our enemy. Segregation, the monster that had terrorized my parents and driven them out of the green Eden in which they had been born, was itself vulnerable and could be attacked, possibly destroyed. I felt as if I had witnessed the first act of a spectacular drama. I wanted to stay around for the second.

Without the miseries of segregation, the South as a homeplace for a Negro of my temperament had clear advantages. In deciding to wait and see how things worked out, I was also betting that progress toward this objective in the Southern region would be more rapid, the results more satisfying, than could be expected in the metropolitan centers of the North, where whites were leaving the crumbling central areas to Negroes while they themselves moved into restricted suburbs and began setting up another kind of closed society.

The second act of the spectacular on which I had focused began with the 1954 decision of the Supreme Court. While this was a landmark, it provoked no wild optimism. I had no doubt that the tide would now turn, but it was not until the freedom movement began to express itself that I felt reassured. We were in the middle of it in Nashville. Our little world commenced to sway and rock with the fury of a resurrection. I tried to discover just how the energy was generated. I think I found it. The singing that broke out in the ranks of protest marchers, in the jails where sit-in demonstrators were held, in the mass meetings and boycott rallies, was gloriously appropriate. The only American songs suitable for a resurrection—or a revolution, for that matter—are Negro spirituals. The surge these awakened was so mighty it threatened to change the name of our era from the "space age" to the "age of freedom."

V

The Southern Negro's link with his past seems to me worth preserving. His greater pride in being himself, I would say, is all to the good, and I think I detect a growing nostalgia for these virtues in the speech of relatives in the North. They talk a great deal about "Soulville" nowadays, when they mean "South." "Soulbrothers" are simply the homefolks. "Soulfood" includes black-eyed peas, chitterlings, grits, and gravy. Aretha Franklin, originally from Memphis, sings, "Soulfood—it'll make you limber; it'll make you quick." Vacations in Soulville by these expatriates in the North tend to become more frequent and to last longer since times began to get better.

Colleagues of mine at Fisk who, like me, have pondered the question of staying or going have told me their reasons. The effective young Dean of the Chapel, for example, who since has been wooed away by Union Theological Seminary, felt constrained mainly by the opportunities he had here to guide a large number of students and by the privilege of identifying with them. John W. Work, the musicologist and composer, finds the cultural environment more stimulating than any he could discover in the North. Aaron Douglas, an art professor, came down thirty-four years ago to get a "real, concrete experience of the touch and feel of the South." Looking back, he reflects, "If one could discount the sadness, the misery, the near-volcanic intensity of Negro life in most of the South, and concentrate on the mild, almost tropical climate and the beauty of the landscape, one is often tempted to forget the senseless cruelty and inhumanity the strong too often inflict on the weak."

For my own part, I am staying on in the South to write something about the changes I have seen in my lifetime, and about the Negro's awakening and regeneration. That is my theme, and this is where the main action is. There is also the spectacular I am watching. Was a climax reached with the passage of the Civil Rights Act of 1964? Or was Martin Luther King's addressing Lyndon B. Johnson as "my fellow Southerner" a turning point? I would rather think that the bend in the road came when President Johnson gave his "We Shall Overcome" speech before Congress, identifying himself with the language as well as the spirit of the common cause. Having stayed this long, it would be absurd not to wait for the third act, and possibly the most dramatic.

X

The Ever-Ever Land

◆

by JONATHAN DANIELS

Nothing is now more precious in the South, so long supposed to be clinging to legends of the past, than myths about tomorrow. Across the century since surrender the region has always needed the romanticized recollections of great days gone to sustain its dignity in poverty. Now it desperately requires what may be a new mythology of unequaled economic advance.

The old agrarian South which fell before the rising industrial North a hundred years ago has sometimes seemed to have as its latter-day spokesman such a nation-stomping segregationist as Governor Wallace of Alabama. Change, Wallace said, was not going to come through *his* schoolhouse doors, but the South had become, he declared, "the industrial mecca of the Free World." Some outsiders, with different ideas about a Free World, have seemed shaken by the speeding industrialization of Dixie. One such Yankee witness was John F. Kennedy. "Every month of the year," he once said as Senator from Massachusetts, "some New England manufacturer is approached by public or private interests offering various inducements to migration southward. Other manufacturers warn their employees that they must take pay cuts to meet Southern competition or face plant liquidation."

Later, as President of the entire nation, Kennedy could see this situation, not as a new North-South conflict, but as a contribution to increasing national productivity. He could rejoice with others, North and South, in such statements as the one in U.S. *News and World Report*: "The Deep South is moving into a new period of stability and growth. A social and economic revolution, twenty years in the making, now is coming of age."

Few have even contemplated, however, the economic paradoxes in the South as a whole. Certainly Samuel I. Newhouse, the greatest collector of newspaper properties in America today, considered the region a rich market when he paid more for the two New Orleans papers than Thomas Jefferson did for the Louisiana Purchase. Yet from the Gulf to the Potomac and to the Ohio, the South still remains the American region of lowest per capita income, least education, and most limited hope. Few who hail the new industrial South have paused to consider that 1964's roar of rioting in Northern cities might have been the extension of the despairing cry which came from deserted Southern villages and the emptier fields around them—the new, new, ever new South.

Historically there is hardly a more frayed fantasy than that embodied in the phrase, "the New South." Credit for it generally goes to Henry Grady, editor of the Atlanta *Constitution*. There was praise at home and abroad for Grady in 1886 when he eloquently hailed the true reunion of the nation and asked for the same kind of industrial development that the region now seeks. However, he spoke shortly before the great depression of the 1890s flung the South back into even deeper poverty than it had known before. Further, the efforts in those hard times of white men and black men working together in radical Populist politics to escape their difficulties led only to greater rigidities of segregation.

An earlier leader who engaged himself in the creation of a new South when it was desperately needed was Edmund Ruffin, gentleman farmer of Virginia. The "Old South" already seemed over when Ruffin came to the management of his ancestral acres on the James River in 1813. More than a century of exploitation of the land in tobacco farming had left the soil washed-out, much of it covered with briers and brush. George Washington's Mount Vernon was becoming an agricultural ruin. Thomas Jefferson, who considered himself the agrarian philosopher, was trying in vain in his debt-plagued old age to find a purchaser for his lands who would pay enough to meet his liabilities. Nobody wanted Southern seaboard land. And from Virginia's barren ground "an emigrating contagion resembling an epidemic disease" spread among the people. Those planters who did not move to fresh acres in the frontier Southwest were beginning in reluctance, sometimes in shame, to sell their "people"—their surplus slaves—to this new Deep South.

Ruffin, though at first regarded as foolish by his neighbors, discovered that the worn soil of the older South could be revived by the application of common fossil shells. After amazing success with his own land, in 1833 he began to preach his methods to others. The land values of Tidewater Virginia increased by millions of dollars. Ruffin was called to South Carolina, where similar wonders were required. He was serving an old land but he wanted—as some do now—not only a revitalized South but one separate and secure in its own ideas.

Slavery seemed to him natural, good for man and master; he was eager far earlier than most of his neighbors for secession. He prophesied a short, devastating war in which the South would suffer from a blockade but Northern merchants would become bankrupt, their cities overwhelmed by mobs of "undigested foreigners." The West, he predicted, would break with the North and join the South. The end he saw was a South—a "New South" of course—rising to vitality in independence, adding industry to its agriculture and trading directly with Europe.

Ruffin preached his dream like a man calling for a crusade. As more Southerners came to his extreme views, Charlestonians gave the Virginian the honor of firing the first shot at Fort Sumter. Afterwards, of course, he saw his fantasy fall apart; his prophecy came only to unbearable prostration. Just a century ago in 1865, two months after Lee had surrendered, Ruffin killed himself on a planta-

tion he had brought from infertility to plenty—and at last to pillage
by Union soldiers who scrawled insulting words on his walls.

No such violent shattering of a dream is in prospect now. Reluc-
tantly Southern politicians who proposed to close the schools rather
than submit to integration have recognized that this would have been
secession, not from the Union, but from civilization. Also, the understanding grows in the South that in the event of a new secession by
South Carolina, no brief defense of Fort Sumter would be necessary.
It would suffice to close the Charleston Navy Yard.

Welcome to Carpetbaggers

Never before has there been such a welcoming, with bands and
banquets, of carpetbaggers. Some of these Yankee newcomers are
gentlemen of a kind that any region would be happy to have; others
are characters eager only to find out how little they have to pay for
the sewing of a shirt. Some have been ready to bite the hands of those
who beckoned them. And, as always, some native Southerners still
operate on the theory that a Yankee is worth more than a bale of
cotton and twice as easy to pick.

This kind of courtship of outsiders did not begin in the South,
though it is as old there as post-Civil War campaigns to "bring the
cotton mills to the cotton fields." Other states and communities,
North and South, were seeking such industry long before Governor
Hugh White of Mississippi provided a sort of model by launching his
"Balance Agriculture with Industry Plan" in 1936.

White was a pudgy old-time lumberman who, after the fashion of
his craft, made stumpy deserts of the forests he stripped, never
dreaming of the modern miracles in woodland care and woodland
profits from which Dixie benefits now. He wanted industry not only
to supplement a lopsided cotton-growing economy, but also to take
the place of shut-down sawmills where all the trees had gone. His
BAWI plan was frankly based upon an appeal to Northern industry to
run away from troublesome Northern unions to the promised docility
of low-wage Southern labor. People were ready to be docile for very
little in Mississippi in the 1930s, when the average per capita

spendable income in White's own county was $198 a year. The first plant he got had previously been hiring convicts in Wisconsin. Free men were cheaper in Mississippi.

Seldom is the appeal quite as crude as when Hugh White stated it, although some folks in Mississippi are still not as well quartered and well fed as convicts in Wisconsin. A softer Southern voice speaks in welcome now. More golf courses and magnolia trees, crinolined girls and juleps on the piazza, are offered in advertisements and presentations. Cheaper labor is never entirely concealed. Fortunately, however, much of the South can be more discriminate these days in the kind of industry it seeks. And in paper, chemicals, electronics, space-age industries, and other fields, companies are coming South intent upon productivity, not exploitation.

Now the time comes to count the economic growth.* One enthusiastic source upon which Southern development agencies depend (*The Record of Southern Progress*) reports that from 1939 through 1962 the eleven Southeastern states (in general, the old Confederacy) gained 24,416 new plants providing 1,630,894 new jobs in industry. That is a lot of plants and a lot of jobs, even if in roughly the same period there was an increase of 14,500,000 jobs in states outside the South which have by no means collapsed in the face of Southern competition. Undoubtedly the new industrial jobs in the South have also spread employment in beauty parlors, shopping centers, and the building of the new suburbs. Obviously, however, a lot more jobs are needed.

The reduction of acres in farm programs has been accompanied by a multiplication of farm machines. Automation and organization, both coming late in the South, have explosively altered the area. Not only has country come to town. The movement from the South, particularly of Negroes though by no means of Negroes alone, has been an exodus hardly ever equaled.

* In space-age development some of the South's growth undoubtedly has been given a boost by the presence of persuasive Southerners at the heads of the Armed Services Committees of both House and Senate. Senator Richard Russell of Georgia recently saw the American defense effort threatened by a proposal to close an air base in Georgia. Other Senators would stand guard over the Army basic missile center at Huntsville, Alabama, and, if necessary, at Cape Kennedy in Florida.

Great differences mark the movements in the old Confederacy. Florida, which a century ago the New York *Herald* called "the smallest tadpole in the dirty pool of secession," has become the fastest-growing state in the nation. Ruffin's Virginia has received more and more suburbanites from that centralized government about which Southern politicians, including its own Senator Harry Byrd, complain. In the decade 1950 to 1960 these two states alone gained 1,632,000 people. But the nine other Southeastern states lost 2,712,-000 people to other regions. The Southern need for jobs may be measured by the 1,291,000 who got new ones against the 2,712,000 who left to look elsewhere. The need is even greater than these figures suggest. In the two decades between 1940 and 1960, Southern farm population declined by 7,700,000 people—almost as many of them whites as Negroes. Certainly industry has done little for these agriculturally dispossessed. The great migration still leaves millions behind, economically bereft.

Keeping People Down

The Southern industrial boom, then, has by no means produced bonanza for all. Indeed, the very eagerness to build up industry has often been accompanied by an insistence on keeping people down. Along with the reports of new factories are stories of children in rural counties coming hungry to school. Some landlords, while recognizing the economic virtue of their own subsidies from federal agricutural programs, have prevailed upon county commissioners not to distribute food to the poor from agricultural surpluses; free food might make the colored folks lazy in the limited periods in which their labor is now needed. And every Southern state except Kentucky "protects" its workers by "right to work" laws which, of course, are devices to make it hard to unionize.

As a result, most Southern workers are anything but opulent. In 1964 North Carolina had more manufacturing workers than any other Southern state, but their average wage was the lowest in the South—and in America ($1.60 an hour compared to the U.S. average of $2.58). And manufacturing wages last year were the best in the Dixie economy. The average annual personal income for Southerners in 1963 was $1,820, compared with $2,449 in the nation. Such figures go far to explain the northward migration in recent years.

No cry of "good riddance" will alter the fact that these emigrants leave behind a weaker South. Not only are customers departing and minds and muscles slipping away; the young and best educated leave first and fastest. The emigration also deprives the South of power at the time when some of its politicians bluster the most. In national elections the vote of Harlem is more prized than the vote of Alabama. And in 1960 the states of Arkansas, Alabama, Kentucky, Mississippi, and North Carolina lost a total of six seats in the national House of Representatives and the Electoral College. In terms of Southern power in the nation the result was the same as if South Carolina, the old bellwether of secession, had been dropped into the sea.

This could be a sort of secession by recession. The situation, however, suggests that if the South, a hundred years after defeat, is to grow in greatness, it is time for a different kind of "New South." There are signs of hope.

The migration from the South has slowed. Some imaginative projects have attracted creative people. In North Carolina in the 1950s there was a growing awareness that advancing research about materials and methods was becoming an industry in itself, requiring the knowledge and labors of highly trained technical men. The result was the Research Triangle, with its corners at the intellectual reservoirs of nearby Duke University in Durham, and the two big branches of the Consolidated University of North Carolina in Raleigh and Chapel Hill. In the non-profit Research Triangle Institute there and in the laboratories of private businesses beside it, studies go on in a variety of fields from fibers to computer processes in industry, microminiaturized electronic systems, pesticides, and cancer-retarding chemicals—even the seismicity of the Southeastern states.

The North Carolina Research Triangle is unique only as it was designed by a combination of academic, business, and state officials.

They created a nonprofit institute as a part of a total research complex including industrial and governmental facilities. Somewhat similar institutions exist at Birmingham and Richmond. On the borders of the Southeast are the Southwest Research Institute in San Antonio and Spindletop at Lexington, Kentucky. Proposals in the same field have been made in Georgia, Louisiana, and even Mississippi. All these projects are inspired not merely by the special research preoccupation of this generation in the nation and the world. They are also motivated by an effort to develop new Southern industries less tied to the low-wage history of textiles, tobacco, and lumber products. There is an increasing understanding that just any kind of industry paying any kind of wage is not enough.

The pursuit of industry goes on. In 1962 more than 40 per cent of all the money spent in the nation by state agencies to advertise industrial advantages was spent by Southeastern states. Industry hunters have become the most petted state officials. Eager politicians join in their quests for industry—often called "raids"—in other states. North Carolina's former Governor Luther Hodges, until recently Secretary of Commerce and now the new chairman of the board of the Research Triangle Foundation, organized and led a safari of businessmen and boosters to Europe, ready if they could to move the Saar to the South. Hodges was also glad to have his picture taken for national publication while putting on a pair of drawers from a manufacturer wise enough to make his underwear in the Tar Heel State.

Other, Wiser Men

There is a South which is neither in the brochures of the promoters nor the news reports of racial violence. The region has not been taught only by demagogues and exploiters. Old Governor Hugh White with his BAWI plan has not been its only prophet. The present South has been shaped, too, by other, wiser men.

There was Howard W. Odum, who came from Bethlehem in Walton County, Georgia. He began his researches in the social sciences long before anyone dreamed of a Research Triangle in North

Carolina. Without the aid of computers he collected as no one had ever done before the significant facts and statistics about the Southern region. No automated procedures since have produced so clear an inventory of the people, the poverty, the promise of the South.

David Lilienthal came as a stimulating stranger to the Tennessee Valley Authority in its first exciting days to harness a river for power, flood control, conservation, transportation, and recreation— and all for people. Here was at last a dream that Odum's brooding statistics could be mobilized to build a more protected, prosperous land. (It is perhaps an irrelevant item in the Southern story that Lilienthal also presided over the use of TVA power in the fission of the atom.) Even now, almost unnoticed, more river developments are planned with local initiative to protect valleys, provide industrial demands for water, and end pollution.

An enlightened concern for people remains too. This concern is shown more and more by younger native politicians not caught in the senility of seniority upon which the South has too much depended in Congress. And at home, court-ordered legislative reapportionment runs against the rule of the rednecks. The Presidential election of 1964 did not so much demonstrate a South broken by civil-rights furies as one in which the majority South declined to be ruled by them.

Younger politicians are facing the facts. They want industry. They know their region's desperate need for it. But basically they want to lift a people to the level of capacity required in a technical age—not merely to attract industry to exploit their limitations. And such men, in a South composed of both white and Negro people, are concerned for the welfare and advance of both races, for a better chance in equal dignity for all. This can still be a hazardous enterprise for a politician. Yet a century after surrender, such concern provides the only hope for a South truly transformed in the achievement of decency for all.

It is not necessary for a Southerner to go back to Civil War times to recognize the contempt with which "po' whites" in the South were once regarded by more fortunate Southerners. They were a recognizable, almost untouchable breed. They are seldom seen anymore.

Beauty parlors at the branch heads have made their girls indistinguishable from debutantes on the streets. The new, almost pathetic eagerness for schools is doing more. Slower but as certainly, improvement in the appearance and the confidence of Southern Negroes is taking place.

But the fact remains that both black and white are still too poor together. Their poverty not only shames a region but threatens the nation too. The South unfulfilled will not stay home in docility.

The Dispossessed

A century is a long time. The Confederate flag is often just confetti in careless hands now. Old Edmund Ruffin's creative labors, twisted by bitterness, only led him to the unbearable sight of Southern catastrophe. Sometimes the work of another scientist, Dr. Charles Herty—in his discoveries about the production of paper from Southern pines which spread the forests to where cotton grew—has seemed only to dispossess people. That is not the present probability. A greener South can be a better South if the tended forests run by the fields to the fringes of the expanding cities. But there must be better places for people in the towns teeming with folk from so many declining rural counties. This almost revolutionary movement from the rural South remains a greater problem than any simple black and white one with which so much Southern and national thought has been preoccupied.

The South may be taught its way to a happier destiny by those whom it has always regarded as its least and last. Sixty years ago my own beloved father, Josephus Daniels, a man who in many ways was regarded as a radical by conservatives in the South and the nation, helped set loose the outcry against a professor who had said that Booker T. Washington was the greatest Southerner since Robert E. Lee. Perhaps I run the risk the professor took. But I think my father will forgive me if I admit the eminence of the Rev. Martin Luther King, Jr. Though in ardor he may run into error, we shall not soon dismiss him. He and others like him have dramatized the antique inequalities Negroes have suffered in Southern and American life.

Yet none but the blind can believe that in the South the unfortunate and the dispossessed are only of one color. Despite the widely advertised gains of the few, the truly New South waits upon the release of the many from squalor and neglect. And on this waits that other long postponed ideal which also has so often seemed pretension —the fulfillment of the American dream.

XI

The Unexpected Dividend

♦

by PHILIP M. STERN

"I think the 1964 Civil Rights Act may turn out to be one of the best things that ever happened to the South. Now that it's the law, the race issue will gradually fade into the background—and that will liberate everyone to begin talking about moving ahead on other things. I think you're going to really see the South blossom in the next decade."

This is no Northern liberal talking, but a lawyer in McComb, Mississippi, which in the summer and fall of 1964 was racked by bombings and burnings. The following spring, like the overwhelming majority of Southern communities thus far tested, it was complying, technically at least, with the operative provisions of the 1964 law.

By the spring of 1965, in the wake of the agonies in Alabama in March, attention had shifted away from the South's response to the 1964 law to the dramatic events of 1965 and the quest for new voting legislation. Significantly, however, the embrace of the civil-rights cause by a Southern President and his advocacy of the strongest voting law ever proposed were received with surprising mildness by Southern Senators. In contrast to the fulminations that formerly greeted all civil rights legislation, some leading Southerners publicly toyed with supporting the new bill, and although only three ultimately did so, the Southerners' 25-day fight in the Senate was described by the *New York Times* as "half-hearted." In mid-March, the *Times* commented: ". . . passage of such a bill, which now seems assured, would have been inconceivable only a year or two ago."

Evidently, then, although Selma captured the national spotlight, a crucial though far less heralded change had already taken place in much of the South during the first eight months of the historic 1964 Civil Rights Act.

In fact, the initial Southern compliance with the public-accommodations portion of that law (the only part that could take hold quickly) was extraordinary. Burke Marshall, until recently head of the Justice Department's Civil Rights Division, said, "Before the passage of the act, I was considered an optimist about how much compliance there would be. As it turns out, I was conservative. The South's performance has been remarkable."

Looking back over the pre-Civil Rights Act period, the word "remarkable" seems apt. In Birmingham, 1963 was the year the police dogs and fire hoses were used to put down Negro protests. By contrast, 1964 saw the peaceful desegregation of hotels, restaurants, and theaters.

In Jackson, Mississippi, 1963 was the year of the Medgar Evers murder, the near-riotous funeral, and Mayor Allen Thompson's famous "armored tank." Few would dare publicly thwart the segregationist Citizens' Council. But not long after the murder of the three civil-rights workers in Neshoba County in 1964, the Jackson Chamber of Commerce, backed by the mayor (an avowed Citizens' Council member) openly called for and won general compliance with the new law.

In Monroe, Louisiana, in the heart of Klan country, a mayor who owed his election to a massive purge of Negro voters openly favored and won substantial compliance.

Most notably, in McComb, so recently ruled by terror, 650 leading citizens publicly called not only for law and order but for racial justice. Negroes were served in previously all-white restaurants.

I by no means wish to suggest that discrimination is dead in the

South or that the region's racial problems are behind it. Especially on the voting front, as Selma so vividly demonstrated, much remains to be done. Even in public accommodations, Negro poverty and established social patterns made the advances to date more symbolic than real, and in small towns and rural areas there was still considerable noncompliance. Although the job-discrimination barrier may have been lowered, the serious gap in education persists. And there were still many towns like Greenwood, Mississippi, locked in a tight segregationist grip, where it was reportedly unhealthy to speak in any but the most defiant terms.

But even in such hard-core areas, the question—at least regarding public accommodations—was no longer *whether* compliance will come, but *when*. Throughout the region the pace of racial progress quickened strikingly in the first eight months of the Civil Rights Act.

Reaction to Inaction

In Birmingham, a sweeping political change was the key to that city's vastly improved racial climate after the riots of 1963. Gone was segregationist Eugene "Bull" Connor as the reigning power; gone, too, the antiquated form of government that gave him his hold. In its place was a more modern mayor-council government, headed by a moderate mayor, Albert Boutwell.

Even before the enactment of the Civil Rights Act, Boutwell resolved that Birmingham must meet any new law with a concerted, planned policy. "The real danger of disorder," he and the Chamber of Commerce jointly warned the city, "will lie in reaching no decision at all." As Congress debated the civil-rights bill, he conferred with restaurant, theater, and hotel owners. By the time the bill became law in July, most of them had decided to comply. Thirty-six hours later prearranged Negro tests began. Police squad cars were stationed out of sight throughout the city. Everything went smoothly. Three hours after the tests began, all the squad cars had returned to regular patrols. Birmingham had passed the test.

This was not Boutwell's only contribution. Soon after he took office, all segregation ordinances were expunged from the books. A biracial citizens' advisory committee was appointed; the people of Birmingham saw on television what would have been unthinkable under the "Bull" Connor reign: Negroes entering City Hall and conferring at the same table with whites about community affairs. A Negro was appointed to the city's important Planning Commission; five of twenty members named to a new antipoverty committee and three out of nine on a housing committee were Negroes. As of early March, 1965, however, the city had yet to satisfy a long-standing Negro request for representation on the police force. Officials said (and some Negroes agreed) that this was in part due to unwillingness among Negroes to apply for or accept police jobs.

The change in Birmingham had its origins in 1961. Business leaders—increasingly aware of the damage done by racial tensions to sister cities such as Montgomery, and of the contrasting prosperity enjoyed by such relatively untroubled cities as Atlanta—began informal discussions with Negro leaders. Significantly, the moving spirit behind this awakening was a prominent realtor, Sidney Smyer, Sr., who was one of the most active organizers of the Dixiecrat party in 1948. In 1965 he flatly declared that the Civil Rights Act "was largely a *re*action to our *in*action in not granting Negroes some of the rights to which they were entitled."

Birmingham voters are apparently enthusiastic about this new look in their city. In December, 1964, they reaffirmed the new form of government by a two-to-one margin.

In early 1965, the racial climate in Tuscaloosa, only fifty-eight miles away, was markedly different from Birmingham's. Headquarters for the United Klans of America, Knights of the Ku Klu Klan, Inc., and hometown of His Lordship, Imperial Wizard Robert Shelton, Tuscaloosa was one of the few Southern cities its size where a number of restaurants initially defied the new law. Although most later admitted Negroes, as of early 1965, government legal action was pending against fifteen establishments.

In 1964, racial tensions in Tuscaloosa were high. The passage of the Civil Rights Act was followed by days of turmoil; street mobs were on the verge of violence. Film actor Jack Palance, who an angry crowd thought had taken a Negro girl into a movie theater, had to be whisked by police not only out of the theater but out of town, leaving his clothes in his hotel and his car on the street, its tires slashed and bearing a sign, "The eyes of the Klan is on you." A mid-1964 impasse over the hiring of Negro bus drivers left the city without a transit system. There were Negro boycotts of downtown stores, and a Negro march protesting the segregated washrooms built into the new marble-and-glass courthouse.*

The strong business and government leadership enjoyed by Birmingham was largely missing in Tuscaloosa. Moderates in the business community generally remained unorganized after the passage of the Civil Rights Act. Mayor George van Tassel is a former New Yorker; there are those who believe he feels he must "out-South the Southerners."

By early 1965 all the city's hotels and some restaurants had integrated, and some of the hold-out restaurants gave the impression they were only waiting for a court order to desegregate so that they could tell their clientele they had no choice. Yet there was almost no communication between the white and Negro communities, and most observers felt that racial harmony would be a long time coming.

Losing the Second War

Compliance with the law in Monroe, an urban island in northern Louisiana's toughest Klan country, appeared to spring from two factors: the unwillingness of the city to allow racial strife to jeopardize its burgeoning prosperity, and the landslide election of Lyndon Johnson.

Unlike Birmingham, Monroe underwent no sweeping political change. The mayor, Jack Howard—the 1964 state co-chairman of Democrats for Goldwater—was elected in 1956; he acknowledges that he gained office because of a substantial purge of Negro (and some white) voters. Obviously proud of his transformation of a debt-

---

* Because of a court order, however, the racial signs were removed and Rooms 132 and 136 of the courthouse are now duplicate, side-by-side men's rooms, paid for by the taxpayers of Tuscaloosa County and open to both races.

ridden city into one eager to undertake major improvements, Howard says people in Monroe are aware of the troubles racial unrest has brought to other cities. "Monroe is moving and growing and it isn't going to stop."

Compliance in Monroe was not immediate, as it was in Birmingham. Restaurateurs were divided as to what course to follow. None wanted to be the first to serve a Negro. This reluctance was intensified one summer evening in 1964 when five hundred apparent Klan sympathizers descended en masse on one restaurant, filling all the seats to prevent any Negro from testing the law. It was a tense and frightening evening for the proprietor, who could not even persuade police to send a squad car to investigate the strange sit-ins.

From July to November, the policy of hotels and restaurants was to deny service to Negroes. Klan sympathizers roved the streets in cars recognizable by their special radio aerials and their stars-and-bars license plates. One downtown store was picketed by Klansmen who heard the lunch counter was to be desegregated; the store was closed for the day.

A monolithic pro-Goldwater sentiment gripped the city. An LBJ bumper sticker was heresy; one Negro was stopped by police who stripped the sticker from his car and arrested him for drunken driving. Many of the leading Goldwater supporters are said to have actually convinced themselves that their man would be the next President. When Lyndon Johnson won by a record-breaking landslide, "they were shaken, really shaken," one Monroe man told me. "Before the election the Civil Rights Act was the law of the country, but not of Louisiana. After the election, it was clearly our law, too." A downtown hotel owner, who admitted he might have gone on denying admission to Negroes "if it had been a real close election," reversed his policy. "With that landslide," he said, "I had no choice."

Apparently the restaurateurs agreed. They met with the Chamber of Commerce and the mayor, and, with the backing of both, let it be known they would accept Negroes.

While in early 1965 compliance was widespread in Monroe itself, the same did not hold for the surrounding rural areas. One café in nearby Jonesboro (population 3,848) denied service to Negroes.

Another gave them menus listing coffee and Coke for sixty cents instead of the usual dime, and pricing a three-dollar steak at eight dollars. Although the library in Jonesboro was technically desegregated and issued cards to 236 Negroes in one day, the next day the new cardholders found that all the tables and chairs had been removed. But in Monroe itself the atmosphere seemed calm. The Klan was less in evidence and was attracting fewer people to its meetings. The attitude in Monroe may have been summed up by Ouachita Parish Sheriff Bailey Grant: "We've lost the Second Civil War. We're now in the Second Period of Reconstruction. Barry Goldwater was the commanding general of the Second Army of the Confederacy, but he had to surrender at Phoenix. But now it's all over. We don't like this law, but we'll obey it."

The story of Jackson, Mississippi is the story of the waning influence of the Citizens' Council. In 1964 the following events challenged the Jackson Council: First, on the day after the Civil Rights Act was signed, the Jackson Chamber of Commerce (which included some Citizens' Council members) publicly urged its members to comply. Second, the Council's best-known member, the mayor himself, who was always to be counted on in the past as a last-ditch fighter against integration, deserted the Citizens' Council by backing the Chamber and urging compliance with the new law even *before* it had been tested in the Supreme Court. Third, the school board ignored the Council's demand that the schools be closed, and in September the Jackson schools were tokenly desegregated without incident.*

Probably the clearest signal of a change in Jackson's racial and political climate was Mayor Thompson's reversal. Through the years Thompson had consistently held out against every racial change in Jackson until the final word on the final appeal had been handed down by the courts. In July of 1964, he could have taken the same stance, pending a Supreme Court ruling. Or he could have remained

* Eighteen months earlier, Ole Miss professor James W. Silver, in *Mississippi: The Closed Society*, had said he was "frightened by the possibilities of what will happen when four or five Negroes walk into Jackson (or other) schools" under court orders.

silent. He did neither. "I knew I was going to have to go through Gethsemane," he said later, "but I also knew it had to be done."

Although the expected Citizens' Council wrath descended upon him, apparently Allen Thompson had not misjudged the public mood. When a segregationist city councilman, Tom Marshall, floated a trial balloon for a possible political race against the mayor the response was not encouraging, and Marshall again became a candidate for reelection to his lesser post.

"We're Everybody"

McComb, a town of 12,000, is eighty miles south of Jackson on Highway 51. In developments there since the 1964 Civil Rights Act, many find the greatest hope for other communities still ruled by segregationists.

The local newspaper described the reign of terror that lasted through the summer of 1964 and into the fall: "Negro homes were dynamited. Molotov cocktails were hurled at the homes of a white city official and three other white residents. Three taverns were burned to the ground; Negro churches were dynamited and bombed. One white man had household ammonia thrown into his face. Individuals were flogged. Gun blasts were fired into homes and businesses."

Both the business leaders and the city officials were silent. The bombers roamed free.

The break came when Pike County Sheriff R. R. Warren suggested to Oliver Emmerich, publisher of the McComb *Enterprise-Journal*, that reward money, which both city and county boards had refused to offer, could help bring the terrorists to justice. An editorial appeal brought private contributions of more than $5,000 within forty-eight hours. Emmerich decided the time was ripe. He published a series of front-page editorials and began mobilizing community leaders. The first meeting consisted of only four men. By the second meeting the group had grown to twenty; by the third, to forty. ("At that point we had to do some winnowing," one of the original four says, "because we found we had some Klan sympathizers in our midst.") Ultimately, a "Statement of Principles" was published over the signatures of 650 McComb citizens, not merely endorsing law and order, but calling for "equal treatment under the law for all citizens, regardless or race, creed, position, or wealth. . . ."

The statement transformed McComb. The next day many local hotels, motels, and restaurants were peacefully desegregated. The mayor, an ex-chairman of the county Citizens' Council who some believed had been "playing along with the racists," called for orderly behavior during the segregation tests.

The bombers were arrested and placed under suspended sentence—contingent on there being no further violence, whether by them *or by others*—and, as of early 1965, the bombings had not been repeated.

No one contends that the city's racial problems have been solved. As 1965 began, only a few hundred Negroes were registered to vote in the county, and the local registrar said he was unfamiliar with and probably would not put into effect the new literacy provisions of the 1964 Civil Rights Act (a sixth-grade education is supposed to rule out any literacy test). The schools were still wholly segregated; the "white" and "colored" signs remained on the City Hall drinking fountains; and the local Rexall drugstore had turned its soda-fountain lunch counter into a private "club," although as a stranger I was twice served there with no questions asked.

Still, a basic change had taken place in McComb. One of the original four explained it:

Before the 650 spoke up, the people behind the bombings considered themselves patriots, heroes, with public opinion behind them—which is not surprising, because that was the way the politicians had been talking, and no one contradicted them.

But now things are turned around. The "thinking people" of this community—the 650—are in control. No one can be against us: we own the land, the businesses; we're the employers, the bankers, the labor leaders—we're everybody. Nobody can lick us, so they're going to join us.

Many regard this as McComb's lesson for other beleaguered Southern towns: the "thinking people"—starting with just four men and ending up with 650—finally found their voice and took control of their community from a handful of segregationists and terrorists.

This lesson was not lost. In early 1965, a group of influential business-men and civic leaders from all over Mississippi met in Jackson to explore ways of emulating the McComb experience in their own communities.

Any consideration of the South's response to the Civil Rights Act would be incomplete if it failed to take into account the many cities of the Middle and Upper South which integrated their public accom-modations many months before the law required them to do so.

Charlotte, North Carolina, is representative of such cities. (Knox-ville, Memphis, Nashville, and Savannah, among others, might be placed in a similar category.) Here, as in Birmingham and Jackson, a combination of business and government leadership brought about peaceful integration of hotels, restaurants, and theaters—a full year before individual proprietors could claim to be merely obeying the law of the land. Charlotte Negroes have now begun to break into "nontraditional" jobs as store clerks, secretaries, bank tellers; new industries wish to hire more. But the long years of educational dis-crimination have left their mark, and qualified Negroes are some-times more scarce than jobs.

Charlotte also is not without considerable racial problems. Ne-groes are dissatisfied with what they consider token school integra-tion and the continued segregation of teaching staffs. Some feel that the city's housing and urban renewal policies work to the Negroes' disadvantage. Yet Charlotte, with an active biracial mayor's commit-tee of long standing, may have turned a corner.

Paying the Piper

As of early 1965 the returns were not yet all in on the South's response to the 1964 act; only one aspect of that—the public-accommodations portion—had yet been felt to any extent. Histo-rians, in fact, may find it ironic that the public-accommodations section was the lightning rod for Southern opposition during the recent Congressional debate, since its short-term effect on Southern life is likely to be insignificant compared with two other portions of the law that have yet to come into full play.

One is the fair-employment section of the law, and although it was not to take effect until July 1965, firms in each of the cities I visited early in the year had either begun complying or were preparing to do so well ahead of the legal deadline. A survey of companies in McComb, for example, disclosed a general willingness to comply. The McComb Manufacturing Company, a clothing mill, after careful planning with its white employees (many of them women from ordinary troublesome outlying rural areas) had hired Negroes. The transition went smoothly. Both the Mississippi Manufacturing Association and the Jackson Chamber of Commerce had held meetings on the question with their members. In Birmingham, the telephone company had invited its supervisors to discuss hiring Negro operators, and, perhaps because of the advance consultation, received pledges of wholehearted cooperation.

Both white and Negro leaders agree that the problem is likely to center around finding Negroes for jobs rather than jobs for Negroes. As one white businessman put it, "The Freedom Rides won't make a girl a stenographer or a boy a bookkeeper." James Polk, a young Negro leader in Charlotte, argues that years of barred doors are discouraging Negroes from applying for "nontraditional" jobs.

The section of the 1964 law likely to have the most pervasive effect on Southern life—the one which bars federal funds from racially discriminatory state and local programs—was just beginning to come into play in early 1965. (It applies to hospitals, colleges, universities, and research centers as well as to public schools.) Because federal dollars are so ubiquitous, this aspect of the new law offers the greatest lever against discrimination and will be the most difficult for the South to resist.* This became quickly apparent; the Texas Board of Education, within days of being requested to do so, voted to sign the non-discrimination pledge essential to the continuation of its annual $37 million of school aid; Georgia and Virginia followed within weeks. As of late February, 324 Southern colleges and universities—including Ole Miss and the University of Alabama—had signed the pledge. Federal officials feel confident this is likely to be the pattern, a feeling confirmed by a leading McComb citizen who believes even *his* local school board will comply. "After all," he says, "he who pays the piper calls the tune—and Uncle Sam sure has been paying the piper."*

Reducing the Risks

In general, national Negro leaders were pleasantly surprised by the South's pre-Selma reaction to the Civil Rights Act. They seem, in fact, far more impatient with the North than with the South, although as CORE's James Farmer put it, "the millennium has not yet come." The Southern Negro, he says, still faces the difficult problems of breaking voting, employment, and educational obstacles.

Whitney Young of the Urban League feels that educational opportunities will have to be opened to more than a handful of Negroes before he is prepared to throw his hat into the air. "You can't start a man in a mile race when his competitor is already halfway down the track and expect him to catch up." Yet Young sees a change of mind, if not of heart, as the South faces up to its racial problems "more honestly than the North. I think that five years from now, Atlanta will have better race relations than Cleveland," he said.

Roy Wilkins of the NAACP acknowledges that there are still the "sticky areas" of voting, jobs, and schools to be dealt with. But he has been impressed and encouraged by the "change of mood and attitude in the South. Just look at the die-hard areas where there has been compliance: Birmingham, Jackson, Montgomery, Mobile, Columbia. In some of those places, the compliance on public accommodations has been spectacular."

What accounts for the widespread acceptance of the Civil Rights Act?

The principal *articulated* reason is that it is, after all, the law of the land, and must be obeyed regardless of personal feeling. Bir-

* "Two major changes at work to promote a change in the South," the *New York Times* said in a prominent front-page story in March, 1965, "are the Civil Rights Act of 1964 and the $1.3 billion education bill now moving through Congress. A number of Southern school administrators acknowledged . . . that because of these two measures they were in an increasingly difficult quandary."

mingham lawyer James A. Simpson, for example, has deeply felt convictions that the Negro is inherently inferior to the white (in part because of what he contends is a smaller cranial capacity). But now he believes he has no choice but to advise his clients to comply with the law. Jackson's Mayor Thompson, whose former prosegregation stance was based on upholding *state* laws, now defends his call for compliance as merely "upholding the law"—this time a federal law. In Monroe, Sheriff Bailey Grant, who describes Negroes as one-time wearers of breech cloths and rhinos' teeth, says, "Look, we don't like to pay income taxes, but we do. The same goes for this law." On a more practical level, a Monroe restaurateur answered a complaining white customer. "The first time a Negro comes in here I'll call you, and *you* can come and help me throw him out—and *you* can go to jail with me, too." He found no taker.

The defense of complying with "the law of the land" has reduced both the risk and the loneliness involved in dropping the color line. Businesses covered by the law are all on an equal footing; none needs risk lone action. Individuals, too, have found comfort in knowing they are not alone. A Charlotte minister compared McComb in 1964 with Grenada, Mississippi, during the Ole Miss riots in Oxford two years earlier. "At that time," he recalled, "a minister friend of mine in Grenada had exactly four people in the town he could even speak to—and that included his wife. What a difference to be in McComb and *know* there are 649 other people with you."

Whole communities seem to have drawn strength from the successful integration of other cities. One Jackson businessman believes his city's experience paved the way in Laurel, Biloxi, Meridian, and other Mississippi cities. Communities have learned from one another. Birmingham studied what Atlanta and Dallas had done; the Chamber of Commerce of Orlando, Florida, called Charlotte, North Carolina, for guidance; and at least two other Mississippi communities have sent observers to McComb. Burke Marshall calls this a "snowballing effect that could have gone either way. But this time it was *compliance* that became contagious, just as defiance was after the 1954 school decision."

This contrast may suggest that today's use of the "law-of-the-land" argument is a surface manifestation of a deeper change in the South. "After all," Harry Golden told me in Charlotte, "the Supreme Court school decision was the 'law of the land' too, and Southern politicians could have urged obedience then, as they're doing now. But they didn't."

One can sense two changes below the surface between 1954 and 1964. One is a resignation to the inevitable, springing from the ultimate failure of every single device of delay, resistance, or defiance to maintain the status quo. The other is a less articulated awareness that resistance is not only futile, it is *harmful.* Hence the chain reaction has had both a positive and a negative side. Birmingham not only looked enviously at Atlanta, but with apprehension at Mobile, Little Rock, and St. Augustine, where racial turmoil had brought not only terror, but *economic* adversity as well.

High-water Point?

A visitor to the South eight months after passage of the 1964 Civil Rights Act came away impressed with the gains already made, sanguine about the future, but nonetheless deeply aware of the fact that the life of the *average* Southern Negro had been very little affected. Patronage of downtown restaurants, theaters, and hotels had largely been confined to test "teams" and is beyond both the experience and the means of most Negroes. Years of second-class citizenship have made him slow to assert some of the rights he has won. (I saw a city bus rolling through downtown Monroe, its only passengers eight Negroes—all sitting in the rear of the bus.) In many counties he was still denied the vote, still discouraged by the same barriers to jobs and education that existed before the 1964 Act was signed. Any significant lowering of these barriers is likely to be more effectively achieved through the Administration's antipoverty program, its various manpower training programs, and its education program than through the 1964 Civil Rights Act itself.

A historian, however, looking back twenty-five years from now at these months, may perhaps mark them as a time when the Southern business community finally found its voice and began wresting control from defiant politicians. "Before July of '64," one Jackson businessman says, "most active businessmen stayed out of the race question. We let the politicians run the show—they or a handful of rabble-rousers." But now that the businessmen are speaking up, local politicians in many places are either joining or following them.

Without wishing to be overly sanguine, I also believe the historian may note the period immediately before enactment of the 1964 Civil Rights Act as the high-water point of the race issue as dominator and inhibitor of Southern economics and politics. By early 1965 there were already signs that the South's new mood was paying economic dividends. Eastern Airlines told Charlotte businessmen, for example, that the city's successful integration in 1963 helped influence the location of a computerized reservation center in Charlotte. And in Jackson, where a national concern had previously decided against a plant expansion, the city's present racial tranquillity caused the firm to take a second look. "This shows," a Jackson manufacturer told me, "how we have been holding ourselves down with our old traditions."

This is what the McComb lawyer had in mind when he spoke of the Civil Rights Act as "liberating" the South. "We've denied ourselves so much in the past," he said. "When we would start to build a new hospital, there would be a big hassle over whether it would be open or closed to Negroes. So we'd end up not building it. Now there'll be no question. It has to be open. So we'll go ahead and build it." Or, as Harry Golden puts it, "When you draw a line and tell people not to cross it, you spend your life watching the line."

There are signs, too, of a gradual freeing of both Southern politicians and the Southern electorate from their enslavement to the litany of race—signs such as Jackson Mayor Thompson's desertion of the Citizens' Council and the failure of a segregationist to launch a countermovement; the defeat of "Bull" Connor in Birmingham and, more notably, the lack of a local rabble-rouser to take his place; the absence of the race issue in Charlotte's last mayoralty campaign, in spite of serious racial disorders elsewhere in the state at the time. Some of this is due to increased Negro voting in all but the hard-core areas—a process that will undoubtedly be accelerated by the 1965 voting law.

A twenty-year journalistic veteran in the Deep South told me, "This is going to mean a whole new breed of Southern politician. For a century, the racists have been inflicting on the South these fourth- and fifth-rate hacks who could only get into office because they could demagogue on the race issue.

"At first I was very leery when President Kennedy put in the civil-rights bill in 1963. I thought it would tear the South apart again. But as I look at it now, it was a stroke of genius. Nothing else could have freed the South from its preoccupation with the race issue—nothing but a law that everyone would feel they had to obey."

Even though Selma and its aftermath disturbed the relatively placid period following the enactment of the 1964 act, this enthusiasm was still shared, in the spring of 1965, by LeRoy Collins, the former Florida Governor who is head of the federal government's Community Relations Service, charged with helping smooth race relations in troubled communities. "I think," he says, "that the South faces a period of prosperity and progress undreamed of before. Past generations in the South hid from the facts. They hid behind the old 'separate but equal' theory. The present generation is facing the facts, grappling with the problems. But the real glory is going to be with the generation coming up."

Notes on Contributors

ARNA BONTEMPS has been associated with Fisk University in Nashville for more than twenty years. His books include *Story of the Negro*, *American Negro Poetry*, and *100 Years of Negro Freedom*. *God Sends Sunday*, his first novel, reached Broadway in 1946 as *St. Louis Woman*.

D. W. BROGAN is professor of political science at Cambridge and a frequent lecturer at American universities. Educated at Glasgow, Oxford, and Harvard, he is the author of *Politics in America*, *The American Character*, and a recent book of essays, *American Aspects*.

JONATHAN DANIELS, editor of the *Raleigh News and Observer*, is the author of many books and articles. His latest book, *They Will Be Heard*, is a history of America's crusading newspaper editors. He has served in several government positions, including press secretary to Franklin D. Roosevelt and 1948 campaign aide to Harry Truman.

JAMES JACKSON KILPATRICK has been editor of the *Richmond News Leader* since 1949. His books include *The Sovereign States* and *The Southern Case for School Segregation*. He is vice chairman of Virginia's Commission on Constitutional Government.

LOUIS E. LOMAX has written three books—*The Reluctant African*, *The Negro Revolt*, and *When the Word Is Given*, a study of the Black Muslims—as well as numerous magazine articles. He now lives in Los Angeles.

WILLIE MORRIS, an editor of *Harper's Magazine*, was born and raised in Mississippi and studied history on a Rhodes Scholarship at Oxford. Formerly editor of *The Texas Observer*, he has written for *Harper's*, *The New Yorker*, *Commentary*, and *The New Republic*.

WALKER PERCY was born in Birmingham and raised in Mississippi. His novel, *The Moviegoer*, won the National Book Award in 1962, and his essays have appeared in *Harper's, Partisan Review, Sewanee Review,* and *Psychiatry.* He makes his home in Louisiana.

PHILIP M. STERN is a Washington writer, author of *The Great Treasury Raid,* and of the forthcoming photographic book on American poverty, *The Shame of the Nation.* He has served in the Interior and State Departments, and was founder and publisher of the *Northern Virginia Sun.*

WILLIAM STYRON was awarded the Prix de Rome of the American Academy of Arts and Letters for his novel *Lie Down in Darkness.* His other works include *The Long March* and *Set This House on Fire.* He is now writing a novel based on the Nat Turner slave rebellion.

C. VANN WOODWARD is the author of *Origins of the New South, 1877–1913, Reunion and Reaction, The Strange Career of Jim Crow,* and *The Burden of Southern History.* Born in Arkansas, he was brought up in the South, and taught at Johns Hopkins. He is now Sterling Professor of History at Yale.

EDWIN M. YODER, a native North Carolinian, studied at Oxford as a Rhodes Scholar. He was an editorialist for W. J. Cash's old paper, the *Charlotte News,* and he has taught history at the University of North Carolina in Greensboro. He is now associate editor of the *Greensboro Daily News.*

WHITNEY M. YOUNG, JR., is executive director of the National Urban League. His book, *To Be Equal,* was published in 1964.

Index

Herty, Charles, 124
Hill, Lister, 48
Historical Commission of Virginia, 29
Hitler, Adolf, 42, 44, 46, 47, 95
Hodges, Luther, 122
Hood, Thomas, 106
Howard, Jack, 130-131
Howells, William Dean, 100
Hull, Cordell, 97
Hutt, W. H., 46

I'll Take My Stand, 42
Independent Presidential electors, 7
Index Expurgatorius, 39
Individual Liberties, 7
Industrialization, 13, 95-96, 115, 118-120
Institute of Race Relations, Fisk University, 112
Intruder in the Dust, 68
Ireland, 41, 42, 44, 46
Isolation, of the South, 6, 10-11

Jackson, Andrew, 5, 22
Jackson, Miss., compliance with Civil Rights law, 132-133, 135, 137, 138
Jefferson, Thomas, 89, 94, 116, 117
Johns Hopkins University, 22
Johnson, Andrew, 48
Johnson, James Weldon, 109
Johnson, Lyndon B., vii, 10-12, 43, 48-49, 58, 73, 87, 97, 114, 130
Johnson, Paul B., Jr., 43, 77

Keeley Institute, 104, 105
Kennedy, John F., 58, 70, 71, 73, 76, 115-116, 141
Kentucky, 100-101, 121, 122
Killian, Lewis M., 47
King, Calvin, 64
King, Martin Luther, Jr., vii, 11, 50-51, 62, 78, 114, 124
Knights of the Ku Klux Klan, Inc., 129
Knights of the White Camelia, 7
Ku Klux Klan, 7, 77, 97, 127, 129, 130, 131, 132, 133

Labor party (Eng.), 45-46
Lamar, L. Q. C., 76
Leadership, Negro, 61-62, 111
League of Nations, 5

Lee, Robert E., vii, 66-67, 80, 124
Lerché, Robert, 96
Lexington *Advertiser*, 78
Life magazine, 32
Lilienthal, David, 123
Lincoln, Abraham, 42, 48, 72
Lincoln Plan, 8
Literacy test for voter registration, 12
Lomax, James, 54, 58, 64
Long, Russell, 48, 126
Louisiana, 69, 102-104, 122, 130-132, 138
Lynchings, 52-53, 72

McComb (Miss.) *Enterprise-Journal*, 133
McComb Manufacturing Co., 136
Macedonia First African Baptist Church, 53, 54, 64
McGill, Ralph, 10, 71
McKay, Claude, 108
Manpower training programs, 139
Marshall, Burke, 127, 138
Marshall, Tom, 133
Marx, Karl, 44
Mays, Willie, 107
Mencken, H. L., 90, 91
Meredith, James, 67, 70, 76
Methodists, 47, 77
Metoyer family, 103
Middle class, Negro, 60-61, 63, 86
Mill, John Stuart, 94
Millsaps College, 77
Mind of the South, The, ix, 89, 90, 91-99
Mississippi, 6, 44, 47, 48, 60, 66-79, 84, 86, 118-119, 121, 122, 126, 132-135; *see also* Oxford, Miss.
Mississippi: The Closed Society, 41, 132n
Mississippi Economic Council, 78
Mississippi Manufacturing Assn., 136
Montgomery, Ala., march on, vii, 11-12
Morgan, Edward, 73
Myrdal, Gunnar, 3

Nation, The, 97
National Association for the Advancement of Colored People (NAACP), 53, 62, 77, 137
National Citizen's Protective Assn., 7

72

HARPER COLOPHON BOOKS